D0308052

CASUAL✝Y

BEHIND THE SCENES

holby
city hospital
ACCIDENT UNIT

Rachel Silver has written for television and the national press. She worked for several years as a drama script editor, and has since published five books, including two television tie-ins. Rachel lives in London with her son, José.

Acknowledgements

I would like to mention the valuable and generous advice and time given to me by the cast, script writers and production team of *Casualty*. Special thanks to Producer Johnathan Young, Production Executive Paul Richmond, Medical Consultant Peter Salt, Script Editor Harry Oulton, Alan Ayres from Drama Publicity, and Kat Roberts from Picture Publicity who got the cast together for a photo shoot at short notice. Thanks also to Viv Bowler, Sally Potter and Miriam Hyman of BBC Books and to my agent Ian Amos.

BBC Worldwide would like to thank the following for providing photographs and for permission to reproduce copyright material. While every effort has been made to trace and acknowledge all copyright holders, we would like to apologise should there have been any errors or omissions.

Sven Arnovstein: 70 below

Nicky Johnston: 65, 74 below, 116 below

Allen Olley: 69 below

Homer Sykes/Network: pages 8, 9, 23, 26, 49, 53 above and below

The photograph on page 10 appears courtesy of Peter Salt.

All other photographs are copyright BBC.

This book is published to accompany the television series *Casualty* which was first broadcast in 1986. The series is produced by the BBC Drama Department.

Executive Producer: Mal Young

Series Producer: Johnathan Young

Published by BBC Worldwide Ltd,
Woodlands, 80 Wood Lane, London W12 0TT

First published 1998
© Rachel Silver 1998
The moral right of the author has been asserted

All rights reserved. No part of this book may be reproduced in any form or by any means, without permission in writing from the publisher, except by a reviewer who may quote brief passages in a review.

ISBN 0 563 38467 0

Commissioning Editor: Viv Bowler
Project Editor: Sally Potter
Copy Editor: Christine King
Picture Researcher: Miriam Hyman
Art Director: Ellen Wheeler

Designed by The Bridgewater Book Company
Designer: Stephen Parker

Set in 9½ pt DIN Mittelschrift
Printed and bound by Butler & Tanner Limited, Frome
Colour separations by Radstock Reproductions Ltd, Midsomer Norton
Cover printed by Belmont Press Limited, Northampton

CASUAL✝Y

BEHIND THE SCENES

RACHEL SILVER

BBC

Contents

How many people does
it take to film a
series of *Casualty*?
Cast and crew at the
beginning of series 12.

Accident
INTRODUCTION

It was Peter Salt's professional 'performance' in the real world of Bristol Royal Infirmary that led to his long association with the fictional world of *Casualty*, as medical adviser and model for the character of Charlie Fairhead. The moment of dramatic conception for writers Jeremy Brock and Paul Unwin was a particular incident in the hospital. One minute, Nurse Manager Salt was breaking the news of a boy's death to his anguished parents; only moments later he returned to the writers and calmly continued discussing their BBC research. Brock and Unwin realized that there was no lack of sincerity or compassion on Salt's part: the 'act' was genuine. It simply showed how hospital staff, working under enormous pressure, had to be able to switch gear, to deal with the distress and yet to go on functioning as normal.

From such early insights *Casualty* was born, rapidly earning its place as one of television's most popular adrenalin-inducing drama series ever. With its hard-hitting and compelling mix of soap opera and drama, *Casualty*, now in its thirteenth series, continues to move and grip millions of people with its complex, up-to-date plots and vibrant authenticity.

Casualty crew film a fire which threatens to engulf a building in the new series: driven back by the intense heat, emergency services battle to extinguish the flames.

Audiences have always been fascinated by the reality of surgeons at work, and follow the lives of television 'doctors' with an almost alarming intensity. Not only are doctors, with their healing abilities, invested in our minds with a certain mystique, but in watching these dramas unfold we can feel a certain amount of relief that it is 'them', those fictional patients, and not us who need the treatment – though with the added *frisson* of knowing all the time that it could potentially be us.

A hospital is a dramatic laboratory – the world, warts and all, meeting regularly in the doctor's waiting room. For scriptwriters this is something of a gift. They are handed a microscope with which to inspect the grislier fundamentals of life. Into the daily regime of a hospital Accident and Emergency department are thrust harrowing stories of life and death, extreme revelations of love and hate riven by grief and vengeance. Doctors and nurses working on this front-line must deal sincerely and sensi-tively with each desperate tragedy, required by the very nature of their role to remain calm and rational throughout.

To some extent, a career in medicine has always involved acting – developing that cool yet caring bedside manner, while simultaneously making rapid complex assessments. In the many popular medical series over the years, ranging from such early shows as *Doctor in the House* and *Dr Kildare* to *Cardiac Arrest, Peak Practice* and *ER*, it is the actors wearing the white coats and stetho-scopes who have caught our imagination.

Casualty itself works as a popular drama series because of its skilful blending of the two fictional streams of the medical drama and the soap opera, together with the documentary streams of medical science and hospital politics. It works because of the strength of the programme's authenticity: not all accidents can be con-veniently patched up, and staff must consistently cope with the traumas of permanent debilitation, disease and death. As viewers, we care about the characters and about the jobs they are carrying out. The pace of the programme is electric, with crisis after crisis being dealt with in the course of a normal working day or night. Nurses, doctors and paramedics rise to each incident with energetic dedi-cation, and simultaneously struggle to keep up a personal

Just one of the many dramas the *Casualty* staff face each week. Charlie and Consultant Mike Barratt, flown by helicopter to tend an injured youth, perform an emergency operation on a mountainside.

Behind the scenes: a large *Casualty* crew is necessary to film yet another dramatic, realistic and heart-stopping moment.

life while coping with the frenetic pace, the stress and constant exhaustion.

The incidents we see are realistic and horrific. Sometimes our worst fears are realized – unrestrained children in car accidents, domestic fires. The famous airline disaster at Holby City airport was so disturbingly plausible on the eve of my departure for a holiday that I was tempted to switch the programme off. I held my breath while Charlie and his team mopped up and reassured the injured as they arrived at the hospital. The raw mixture of disaster, the detail of medical science and the human drama between the characters, is a miraculous recipe for compulsive viewing.

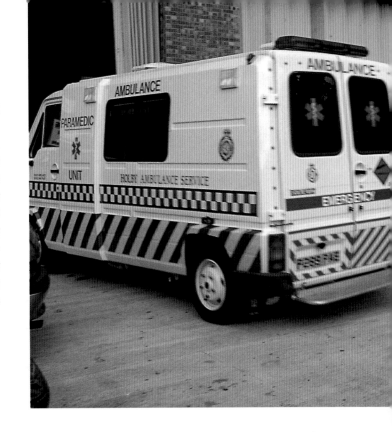

The *Casualty* set is just behind this door. Unfortunately, the only way to get in is to bear a strong resemblance to one of the medical cast.

Senior House Officer Dr Richard McCaig struggles to come to terms with his multiple sclerosis while dealing with the rigorous demands of his job in the busy A&E department.

At the Holby City set the distinction between reality and fiction is blurred: the ambulances look authentic but they wouldn't be much use in a real-life emergency.

The series was originally filmed at BBC Television Centre in London, but once it was established as a clear hit, running weekly for half of every year, a permanent set was created in a warehouse on the outskirts of Bristol.

If you stand outside an anonymous concrete hangar on a bleak industrial trading estate, only the two Holby City ambulances parked outside give you any hint that for over a decade this place has been home to life and death, deliverance and despair, hope and fear. Inside pulses the now familiar world of emergency medicine, brought dramatically to the screen by the exceptional combined efforts of television's creative talent and professional hospital staff, and driven by the immediacy of videotape.

Here we take a look backstage at the actors and programme-makers — not forgetting the make-up and costume designers, the stunt men and women, and the technical staff and film crews — who put together the show that we eventually see. Veteran *Casualty* actor Derek Thompson, who plays Charlie Fairhead, sees the series as 'the village pump where the stories of the world get told. It's to do with issues of the day. It could be the front desk of a cop shop, the green and red channels at customs, or the reception desk at A&E'.

This book looks at how *Casualty* began with a single idea and was developed, through research at a real Casualty department, into a drama series with characters and situations that are, frequently, harrowingly true to life.

Consultation CHAPTER ONE

Once you have become immersed in the fictional world of *Casualty*, it is an unnerving experience walking into the real A&E Department at Bristol Royal Infirmary to meet Peter Salt, Nurse Manager in charge and also the inspiration for the fictional Charlie Fairhead. A passing paramedic in his green uniform could easily be Josh; people on trolleys could casually be dismissed as malingering extras; and a fake wall could, at any moment it seems, be expected to collapse in a heap with the light brush of a passing elbow.

Peter Salt readily admits that sometimes on the *Casualty* set it is hard even for him to tell fact from fiction. If you don't look much above eye level, where all the overhead lighting and sound booms crowd the roof, the line between truth and make-believe could become distinctly blurred.

'Your heart jumps,' says Salt, 'when somebody with a fractured femur leaps off a trolley – until you suddenly remember that it's not real. It all has to look so accurate, even details that may never be seen on the screen. For instance, a hole in somebody's abdomen can never be just a bloody hole – all the internal organs are actually made to look correct.'

The vital Salt has been a potent force in the making of *Casualty* right from the beginning, when the show was based at TV Centre before it moved to Bristol. He recalls a fateful meeting: 'Jeremy Brock and Paul Unwin came with producer Geraint Morris to do some research at the hospital, and I happened to be on duty.' It was a moment that changed his life. 'Geraint asked me if I'd like to look through some scripts for them in an advisory capacity, and it all really started from there.'

Gradually the work escalated. Salt found himself not only looking through scripts, but talking to writers and directors and advising production staff and actors in the studio. But he never gave up the day job. In addition to his work on the TV series, Salt still does his gruelling full-time job – running the A&E Department at Bristol as Nurse Manager. He tries to limit his *Casualty* work to weekends and evenings to reduce any potential criticism of his commitment to A&E.

Salt advising costume designer Maggie Hall on the type of medical equipment which will be needed at a night-time shoot.

'I deliberately do the BBC work in my own time,' he says. 'It just wouldn't be acceptable to me for anyone to say, "Well, we're short of staff today and he's swanning off to the BBC," so I never let the two jobs overlap. Not a day goes by, when the show is filming or being prepared, that I don't get calls from the Beeb. Just this morning, before I came to work, four scripts arrived in the post. Of course they had to be read and checked – preferably yesterday! I do that kind of work at night.'

As Nurse Manager, Salt runs the department as a nine-to-five office job, although he still does some clinical shifts in order not to lose credibility with his colleagues, and to maintain contact with the reality of the medical side of the work. He enjoys the excitement of combining this work with 'mixing with the people from the telly'. But after thirteen years it is no longer quite such a novelty. He knows everybody involved in the show very well now and finds them still good company and receptive to his ideas. He takes great pleasure in what has become a close and very professional working relationship.

Peter Salt is the medical adviser on nursing matters to the television series.

Actor Derek Thompson
as Charlie Fairhead
when he began playing
the role inspired
by Peter Salt
thirteen years ago.

Salt denies being the mirror image of Charlie, but there are certainly overlapping elements in the lives of the fictional and the real men. 'What has happened is that Charlie's career pattern has followed mine,' he says. 'Of course such things as Charlie's love affairs and his famous habit of standing with his hands thrust deep in his pockets are all his own.' Then he adds quickly with a smile, 'I don't do any of that! I simply advise him, and of course we are both now the managers of our respective departments.'

Born in Germany into an Air Force family, Salt lived in Malaysia before going to school in Cornwall. When he left school he briefly worked on a fishing boat before deciding on a career in psychiatry – just like Charlie did. 'Initially I was a psychiatric nurse. Then I moved to Bristol and went into A&E. I never went back to psychiatry, but was promoted through the A&E service instead, although I have at different times worked in other departments of the hospital.'

Derek Thompson, who plays Charlie, no longer feels he has to spend time observing staff at Bristol A&E. He has

RIGHT Each series is renowned for a couple of dramatic accidents which although truly shocking for the viewers must be medically realistic and believable. The 'major incident' at the beginning of series 13 brings Dr 'George' Woodman out into the field to tend the injured.

already covered that ground. What he does do, though, is discuss with Salt the many changes that have taken place over the years in the NHS which might affect Charlie particularly. 'Obviously we consult quite closely about his changing role and work it out together over time,' confides Salt. 'Often it's just a question of his reactions: how would Charlie respond to such and such a situation; might he over-react? Would he have an explosion about it? Or would he just let it pass?'

The format for each series of *Casualty* usually involves a couple of major accidents, normally at the beginning of

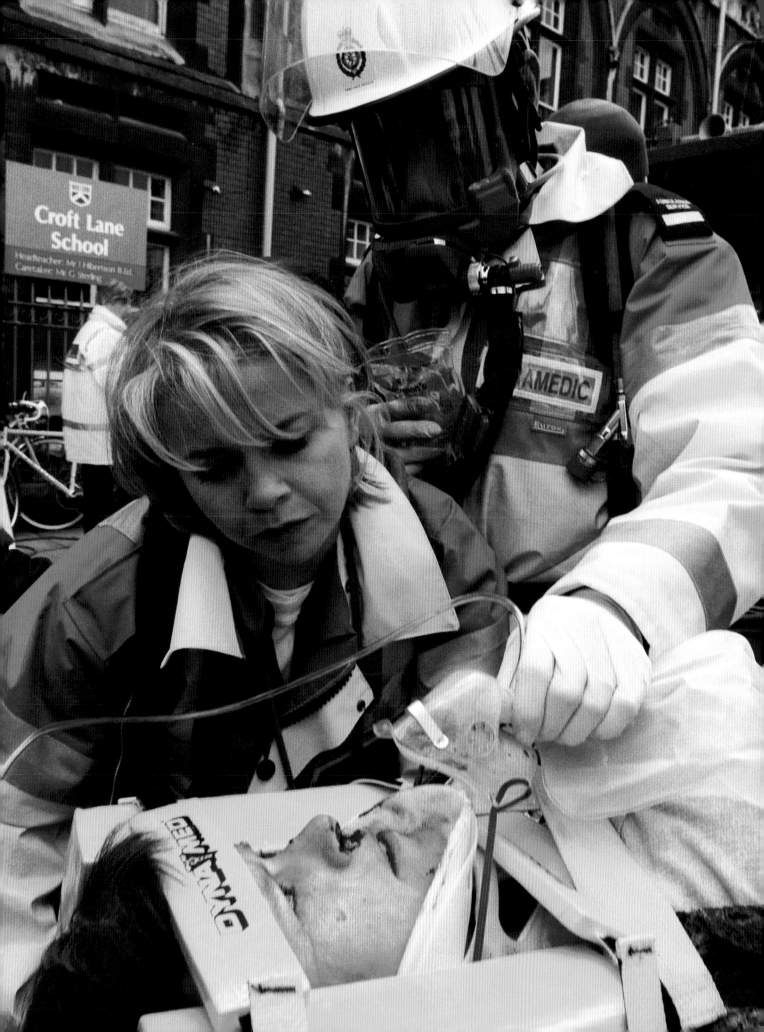

a series, and then another one mid-way through the series in the Christmas episode. Series 12 (1997/98) also began to turn away from pure medical drama and started to concentrate on the personal lives of the regular characters outside their hospital routine.

As the 'Prognosis' on page 92 points out, the plan for the forthcoming series 13 is to push the emphasis emphatically back in a medical direction, reflecting the cut and thrust of a real A&E department. One pioneering episode will follow a shift in A&E entirely from Charlie's point of view. This medical emphasis is no bad thing, according to Salt, who prefers the medical to the soap element of the show. But he acknowledges that the high and fairly regular quantity of medical emergencies in *Casualty* is not actually borne out by the normal routine of his department. 'In reality at Bristol,' he says, 'we could have three major accidents in a week, but equally we could have no major accidents in three years. Unlike the TV

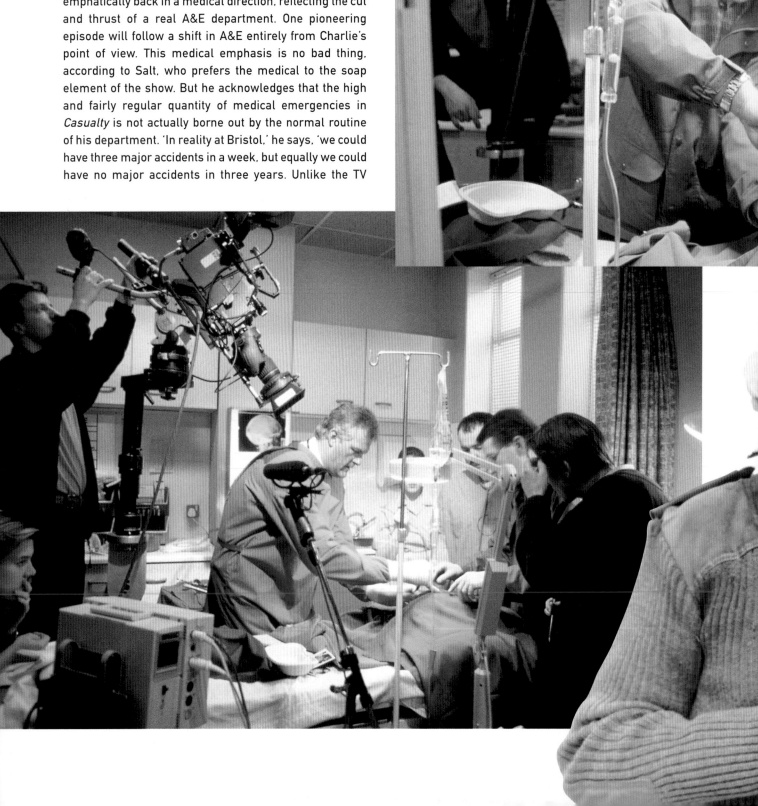

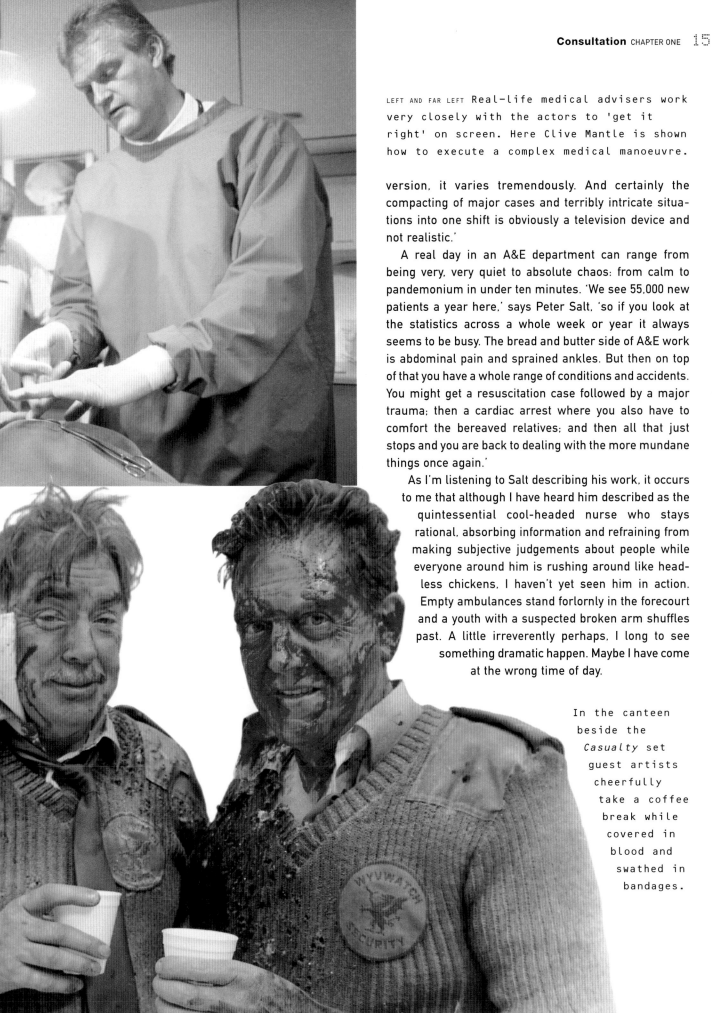

LEFT AND FAR LEFT Real-life medical advisers work very closely with the actors to 'get it right' on screen. Here Clive Mantle is shown how to execute a complex medical manoeuvre.

version, it varies tremendously. And certainly the compacting of major cases and terribly intricate situations into one shift is obviously a television device and not realistic.'

A real day in an A&E department can range from being very, very quiet to absolute chaos: from calm to pandemonium in under ten minutes. 'We see 55,000 new patients a year here,' says Peter Salt, 'so if you look at the statistics across a whole week or year it always seems to be busy. The bread and butter side of A&E work is abdominal pain and sprained ankles. But then on top of that you have a whole range of conditions and accidents. You might get a resuscitation case followed by a major trauma; then a cardiac arrest where you also have to comfort the bereaved relatives; and then all that just stops and you are back to dealing with the more mundane things once again.'

As I'm listening to Salt describing his work, it occurs to me that although I have heard him described as the quintessential cool-headed nurse who stays rational, absorbing information and refraining from making subjective judgements about people while everyone around him is rushing around like headless chickens, I haven't yet seen him in action. Empty ambulances stand forlornly in the forecourt and a youth with a suspected broken arm shuffles past. A little irreverently perhaps, I long to see something dramatic happen. Maybe I have come at the wrong time of day.

In the canteen beside the *Casualty* set guest artists cheerfully take a coffee break while covered in blood and swathed in bandages.

I voice my disappointment to Salt as he takes me round on a guided tour. It transpires that he has in fact had two formal resuscitations before 10 o'clock that very morning but that then things had eased off a little. He confirms the impression I have formed that there is indeed a relationship between the numbers of accidents and the time of day.

'It'll probably peak again after about two o'clock,' he says. 'Then it will be a pretty busy afternoon before it eases off a bit by teatime. The accident level often reflects people's free time, and what they are doing. At meal times, for example, there is often a lull because there aren't many people around. During the school holidays the number of children getting run over suddenly peaks because there are so many more of them around. Unfortunately the school holidays are always very busy.

'Again, at weekends when people are out and about pursuing leisure activities, we get them coming in with fingers cut off while trimming the hedge, lots of sports-related injuries and of course car accidents. If it's busier out and about, we're busier.'

Peter Salt demonstrates airway protection and ventilation to Claire Goose so this can be realistically portrayed in the programme.

In the department I notice that the reception desk is screened by bulletproof glass as in a bank, unlike the more welcoming *Casualty* version where Amy sits doling out sweets to fractious children. Salt points out that there have been too many drug-related attacks on staff to take any risks with personal safety. Only the previous week a crack addict had waved a gun at a nurse and had had to be forcibly removed by the police, fortunately without any injuries.

The hospital in Bristol is located in the centre of the city with up to 400 pubs and clubs and other licensed premises within its catchment area. This obviously gives rise to a lot of night-time activity for the A&E department linked to drugs, alcohol and fights.

In some ways working for the TV programme must provide some light relief for Salt, who still finds it odd to be eating his lunch next to a man with a ruptured spleen hanging out of his abdomen, even though he knows the actors have to keep their make-up on regardless of lunch breaks. 'It can be particularly disconcerting for my medical colleagues who sometimes come on to the set from the real hospital down the road to help me out – they may never have seen the extent of the detailed prosthetics before.'

Most of the equipment on the *Casualty* set is in fact the real thing. 'Ironically,' Salt tells me ruefully, 'the reps are much more happy to give stuff to *Casualty* than to give it to the NHS. I went to a medical meeting yesterday to

discuss the first episode of series 13, which is going to be a "big start", and the AFM [assistant floor manager] who was sorting out the props asked me what kind of monitoring they would need. I told him and he breezily responded, "Oh, we'll need to get another three or four of those then." I sweated blood to get one of those into our hospital here.'

Research is crucial to the programme, to give it credibility, and actors and production staff spend long hours observing in the hospital. Salt arranges this for them because he appreciates the importance of reflecting the jobs of his medical staff and exploring serious issues in a realistic way. He is also pleased that scenes are included demonstrating useful first aid for viewers to absorb, such as how to keep an accident victim lying down to protect the neck, and to treat burns with cold water, as well as pointing out the potential dangers of over-the-counter drugs like paracetamol.

Make-up, costume and design teams all spend time observing in the hospital, as well as the actors. 'They're

Make-up artists spend research time in a real Casualty department to ensure the accuracy of their special effects. Here on location 'blood' is applied, using a fine brush for the gory finishing touches.

not disruptive,' says Salt. 'They're very aware that this is a place of work for us. They pick it all up very quickly. My role as medical adviser goes beyond just telling the actors what size syringe to use: you talk to the whole gang to make sure they all get it all right.'

A treasured *Casualty* memory of 'getting it right' involved Salt playing Megan's (Brenda Fricker's) hands, for a rather complicated medical manoeuvre. 'I wore extra-long gloves in an attempt to hide my hairy arms,' he recalls with amusement, 'but I was still in shot and was eventually reduced to making a glamorous appearance in that particular episode in a nurse's dress.'

Pre Op. CHAPTER TWO

Research

A huge amount of work goes into *Casualty* before the actors speak a word – or before even a word is written. The watchword for the series is authenticity, which requires scrupulous and far-reaching research.

Long-time researcher and then script editor on *Casualty*, Harry Oulton, tells the story of when he first spent a day observing the action in a real Casualty department. He witnessed a death and felt like a dreadful intruder. A man in his forties had suffered a heart attack and collapsed. Medical students tried to revive him with CPR; but then the consultant told them to stop and 'called' time of death. 'The students melted away,' recalls Oulton, 'and there was just a man lying on a bed – dead. It was so powerful. Then his wife came in, she was completely distraught. It was terrible, I felt like a voyeur. If she had known I was from *Casualty*, taking notes, she would have been horrified.

'You hope that such poignant events will inform the way you communicate your own feelings and emotions to the

Camera crew film ambulances arriving to collect the injured from the bombed Holby shopping centre.

Writers always have to bear in mind the practical and budget constraints involved in filming the story — a lot of work goes into even the simplest scene.

script writers. That's why we send all our writers to Casualty departments, to spend a day there and develop respect for hospitals and for human life.'

Oulton was, in fact, thrust suddenly and involuntarily into the fictional A&E world from an impressionable age when his sister, Caroline Oulton, was appointed to research the very first series of *Casualty* in 1986. 'She was quite involved with developing the original concept with Jeremy Brock and Paul Unwin. I met Peter Salt at the same time.'

Oulton is an enthusiast. His face lights up immediately when asked to describe his job. He relishes the detail. 'I had to learn very fast: the different kinds of cardiac arrest; what can go wrong with people; what can and can't happen. In this job I also filter out actual accidents that are too rude to go on television. Any nurse you talk to will say, "The number of strange objects we have to remove from people's rectums is extraordinary. Why do you never show that?" We're a pre-watershed show so we can't really feature that sort of thing.'

Tensions at Holby City:
Charlie and Eve don't
always see eye to eye.

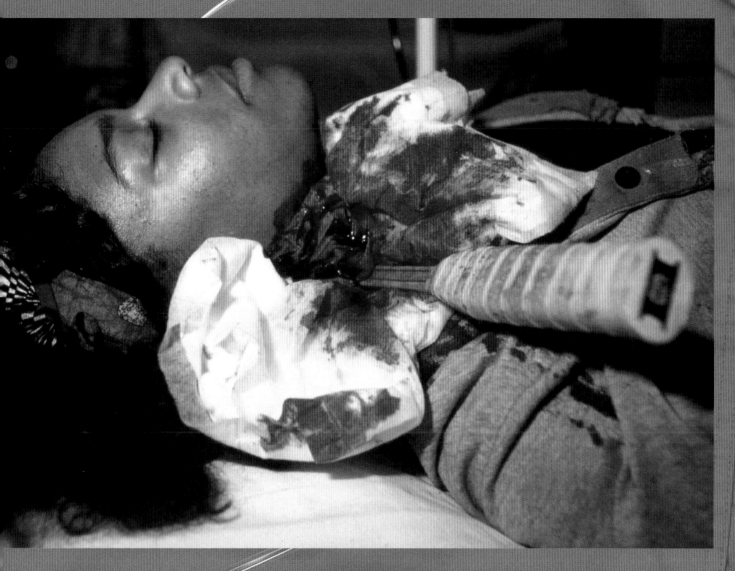

Realistic gore is part and parcel of a hospital series. Here a young woman is operated on after slipping and injuring herself on a broken squash racket in one of *Casualty*'s more bizarre moments.

Casualty did run post-watershed for one series, when a darker feel was introduced, but it was subsequently decided to move the show back to the family viewing time of eight o'clock. 'Cynically speaking, there was nothing to be gained from excessive gore.'

Oulton maintains that it is because the storylines seem so much about real people's lives that the 'it could be me' factor comes strongly into play; and that is what makes the show so popular. 'Quite apart from the soap opera elements where you get to know the doctors – your favourite characters – and you love them, love seeing them married, there is also the aspect that you're watching television and meeting totally alien people. You hold your breath wondering what's going to happen. You think, "I know something nasty is going to happen!"'

Unlike other medical series, such as *ER*, which are mainly studio-based, the *Casualty* filming schedule involves one week on location followed by one week in the studio. Three or four stories are established in each episode and the audience watch them evolve. You get to know the people involved. Then they have an accident and get rushed into Casualty where the story is resolved. This could only happen in an A&E department where the turnover is so rapid. The staff have to deal with many separate incidents in each shift.

Part of the script editor's job involves talking to people and finding out what they like about the series. 'I was talking to someone last night, for instance,' elaborates Oulton, 'who said his wife loved the soapy stuff. She loves to see the doctors and nurses getting on or bickering, while he personally loved all the "God, what's going to happen to them?" bits, and trying to guess the accident.'

During the episode in series 12, in which Tina talks about her rape ordeal, Oulton explains that the problem of what could be shown to a pre-watershed audience, including children, was all to do with responsible handling. The rape itself was not shown. 'You show things which you believe are dramatically powerful, issues you want to deal with. What is important is the way you handle them. You have to be sure to do it in a responsible fashion so as not to cause extreme upset. You're trying not to make people feel excessively harrowed; but you are still presenting them with real-life events.'

Casualty deals sensitively with the subject of rape when Sam notices that the uncharacteristically moody Tina has severe bruising to her wrist. Later she tells Eve about the attack.

Casualty is very true to life, and the story lines painstakingly researched. There are three medical advisers on call at all times: as well as Peter Salt, the nursing adviser, there are Dr Phil Coburn and paramedic Clive Hadrell. Advice is given on administrative and medical procedure, but the advisers also suggest stories for future plots.

'Basically,' says Oulton, 'they tell us where we're going wrong and when we're getting it right: what we can do, and what we can't. Whether we can drive an ambulance into a burning building, or whether that's a really ridiculous idea. They keep us on track. But there's still a constant affectionate battle between us where we're saying, "No, no, no we want to do that dramatically," and they protest,

The director Alan Wareing (left) checks the authenticity of a storyline with real—life charge nurse Nigel Wilkins (centre) at Bristol Royal Infirmary.

saying, "Well, that would never actually happen."'

The research Oulton did last year involved the traditional twin elements: the ongoing serial agonies of the medical staff interspersed with the guest stories. 'There is a lot of preparation for the serial element which ideally we do before we start filming. For example, if you're doing a story about gambling you find out in detail how that works, or how rape victims feel, to add credibility for the long-running story we did on rape. We also did

After witnessing a man engulfed
by flames during the big
motorway pile-up, General Manager
Elliot Matthews suffers from
post-traumatic stress (the 'big
issue' dealt with in series 12).

four episodes about post-traumatic stress. Elliot, the General Manager, was very traumatized by a terrible incident in the Christmas special. We took him through post-traumatic stress in the work place, how that manifests itself, and how it would be resolved. To do that I had to talk to the head of Trauma and Generic Counselling at London Transport. They get a lot of people throwing themselves under trains, and they have had a lot of employees who can't cope with that and who cannot even physically drive the trains any more. I looked at how they deal with their trauma, and their attempts to cope and come through it all.'

The overall story in terms of what happens to the main characters throughout a particular series is plotted in advance by the producer and script editors. It is then divided up so that you get the major 'beats' (or themes) of each story, which are distributed to as many as twenty writers. The writers then come up with their guest stories, which should interplay with what is already going on. The two elements help to drive each other along. The writers use the serial element to tell the guest stories, and the things that the guest characters are experiencing mirror or reflect obliquely what the regular characters are going through. 'We did an episode on surrogate motherhood, for instance, at the time when Jack, who was the Consultant, had been left by his pregnant fiancée. She didn't want Jack to be involved in the upbringing of their child because she didn't want anything more to do with him. So into that situation we brought in somebody who was a surrogate mother, who had not wanted to give up the child. As a direct consequence we had Jack react particularly badly, seeing her behaviour as very selfish. Basically we are paralleling his life but slightly obliquely. We use one story to tell the other, and we use one to play off the other.'

Consultant Jack Hathaway quits Holby City to pursue his pregnant fiancée Jayne.

Before arriving on our screens, a vast amount of work has already been completed: all props are accurately researched and are in large storage cupboards on set. The set dresser is supplied with medical items (such as stethoscopes and body bags), twenty or so extra phones and even lottery tickets to recreate an authentic hospital scene.

Actual day-to-day detailed research of a story involves a collaborative process between researchers and writers. A writer might want to do a story about a prisoner, so the researcher will have to go to a prison and talk to people there about the nitty-gritty of prison life. 'Ideally,' says Oulton, 'they [the researchers] try to do that for themselves, but if they're pushed for time then I help out. Often I will do some research and they will also do some; then we ring each other up and talk about it. They'll talk to their script editor, and out of that we get our story and exactly how they want to tell it.'

Alternatively, there are more complicated pieces of research. In the 1987 Christmas episode something appropriate was needed such as a birth. But there was a problem. There had already been a baby, in episode 1, born in the back of an ambulance. So they decided instead on a story involving a dairy farmer in which calves could be born. Oulton picks up the story. 'The producer wanted me to find a type of cow which could realistically have calved at Christmas time! Just to add a further spin we had to film the episode in October, so we needed the calf then. I had to find a type of cow that could calve five months before the normal time so that we could film it in time for our transmission date. I rang the National Dairy Association and cried, "Help!" Luckily there was one type of cow that could actually do it. I found the relevant farm, close to Bristol, and told the director that there would be three or four calves born at the right time. Then as happens in telly all the time they suddenly decided that the character was going to be a sheep farmer instead. No births needed. They would just give the farmer a wagonload of hay to unload!'

The Writers

Of the dozens of writers who have contributed to *Casualty* over the years, two of the most enduring have been Barbara Machin and Peter Bowker. Their views, I feel, offer a clear indication of how and why *Casualty* works. To counterbalance their long experience, I also spoke to new recruit Andy Rattenbury, who brings a fresh eye to the series.

From her Cotswold hideaway, Barbara Machin stresses the importance of the Kleenex factor. 'Making people cry is important,' she maintains sternly. 'The stories have got to be real.' To that end, the first thing she does when researching an episode is to put on a white coat and spend a twelve-hour shift in a hospital A&E department.

Machin often does the big set-pieces for *Casualty*. Last year she wrote both the double-length Christmas special and the grand finale of the series – Baz and Charlie's wedding extravaganza. Starting work on 'The Golden Hour', the Christmas special, Machin was faced with the classic problem of a big episode: she needed a big dramatic event. She decided eventually on a 'good old-fashioned motorway pile-up, because spectacular aeroplane and train crashes had been done before'. She paid a visit to Moreton-in-Marsh Fire College, 'the university of fire', to get advice on how best to create a gigantic fireball. When it came to actually filming the episode they could not get permission to create the accident on any real road, and eventually found an airfield south of Swindon where the team could stage the catastrophe in peace.

Technicians record the happy event in Barbara Machin's end-of-series wedding story. Charlie, Baz and best man Ash arrive at the local marina in style.

'I used the crash as a sort of Trojan horse,' she explains, 'to be a sort of organic centrepiece.' Then into the crash she wove a series of stories. One was about a woman in a destructive relationship driven to take slimming pills to please her lover. Unable to see properly as a consequence, she skids into some traffic cones, causing other cars to crash around her. But this is only the beginning of the débâcle. Into this, Machin worked in an under-age sex story. A fifteen-year-old girl is sleeping with her sixteen-year-old stepbrother, which causes terrible ructions within the family. The two youngsters have slipped off together to a party; *en route* they argue and swerve into the crash. A third story involves a man, the sheep farmer, moonlighting as a lorry driver, who is tragically burnt to death in the motorway pile-up when he crashes into a builder's lorry carrying propane canisters. Yet another strand involved a car which crashes into the whole mess, driven by a girl who, we later discover, has been dating gay nurse Sam's boyfriend. Clearly some of the storylines get quite complex. In this case, the tricky part for Machin was trying to maximize the effect of how all these stories could knit together in a believable and dramatic way.

Machin does a significant amount of her own research, and is particularly interested in using issue-based stories. In one episode she included a story about a man who took a paracetamol overdose. 'It was a contentious issue that needed an airing and provided a strong story.' In her story the suicidal man changed his mind about wanting to die, but had not been aware that the effects of a paracetamol overdose on the liver are irreversible and fatal.

This is the sort of fact, Machin contends, that should be more widely known. Other issues she has addressed include a transplant story, and the subject of euthanasia which is a grey area she dealt with four series ago and will be coming up again in the new series. For her part she firmly believes that preserving someone's life at any cost is not necessarily the right thing to do. 'I hope that when it comes to my turn I get a medic who knows that.'

When junior nurse Jude was stabbed at the end of series 11, Machin looked at violence in the Casualty department and how it affected all the other characters. There was also the problem of the stabbing being blamed initially on the Care in the Community patient, Aztec Ken. This created a storm of controversy, despite being an obviously fictional case. Machin sees it as one of the problems of writing for *Casualty*. 'If it's done well, it's provocative and educational. The stories are of life in extremis. The unending appeal of the series is that it is not too far from your own life.'

MAIN PICTURE A builder's lorry carrying propane canisters explodes in spectacular fashion when it collides with the farmer's truck in the motorway pile-up in *Casualty*'s 1997 Christmas special.

FAR LEFT Sam, George and Mark look on horrified.

INSET *Casualty* staff attending the scene of the accident rescue a woman from her flashy four-wheel-drive and treat her bleeding cuts. This leads to her shocking revelation that she shares the same boyfriend as Staff Nurse Sam.

Chronology of Writing an Episode
as explained by the scriptwriter Barbara Machin

- Research in an A&E department

  — you're constantly looking for new stories.

- Write up story ideas, then the team and medical experts choose with you.

- Write a scene-by-scene breakdown.

- Check each story is a detective story, with constant tension.

- Add in the regular characters and their stories,

  integrating the guest stories.

- Write up all scenes on postcards and put them out on the kitchen table,

  and do a jigsaw until it works.

- Send to medical adviser.

- Everything is looked at from both a dramatic and a medical point of view.

- Do several drafts.

- The director comes on board and makes his or her changes.

- 'A scene you have written with floodlit hockey and an accident

  becomes a punch-up in someone's garden.'

- 'You go and watch it and warm your hands on something that

  started on a cold night in Bristol A&E Department.'

Firemen attempt to put out the fire of a petrol-bombed ambulance in 'Boiling Point'.

A *Casualty* script writer since series 8, Peter Bowker was introduced to me as the man who wrote the most contentious episode ever. In 'Boiling Point' he famously had a rampaging mob of rioting youths burn down the hospital. Netting an audience of seventeen million, the highest viewing figures *Casualty* had ever had, the episode also caused a record number of complaints. 'The odd thing about it,' muses Bowker, 'was that at the time everyone had an opinion about it, whether or not they had seen it. But one good thing about it was the number of young people who wrote in and said they weren't going to burn down hospitals.'

Patients are herded outside for safety after rioting youths attempt to burn down Holby City.

As the fire at Holby City continues to rage, patients are tended to outside in the car park.

Duffy and Charlie look on as the hospital burns: is this the end for Holby City?

In reality Bowker comes across as a rather mild Yorkshireman, who now lives in London. He explains that 'Boiling Point' was conceived as a combination of something personal he wanted to write about, and also a way of giving an end-of-series episode maximum impact. At the time he was living on an estate in Leeds and found that mindless indiscriminate violence on the part of young people caused him, a self confessed non-violent liberal, to start sleeping with a tyre iron by the bed. The episode was written on a wave of anger and a sense of shame at how the vigilante mentality can take hold of you.

Bowker has been a professional writer for six years, but only gave up his job as a special needs teacher three years ago. 'I'd been writing in my spare time and getting rejection slips for ten years. I decided to see if I could be a professional writer and took an MA, remortgaging my house. I quickly realized I wasn't a novelist and so changed to screenwriting, which was like coming home because I understood TV.' He got his first break when he sent the script of a play to a script editor at the BBC and it was passed on to *Casualty*.

His first story idea was about a boy at the hospital where he taught. 'There was a young man who had his behaviour very well controlled with a certain medication, which meant he could live safely in the community. Then they found out that the medication was actually reducing his platelet count to a dangerously low level. The choice was whether he should have a contained life, or take the drugs which would help him but have a terrible medical effect.'

The first episode he wrote was wildly ambitious. 'It had everything in it. It was really not an episode of *Casualty* at all but a play by Peter Bowker. It was me up there, not the regulars. That's just a learning thing. Learning how to accommodate your style and concerns into a series. People don't turn on for a script by Peter Bowker, they turn on for Charlie. Once you batten down your ego then you can write.' That was series 7. He then went on to write episodes in most of the series to date.

Bowker did not find his research at the A&E Department of Leeds Royal Infirmary particularly helpful – although, he remarks, it was disturbingly easy to put on a white coat and trail somebody. 'I think because I had taught special needs in a mentally handicapped hospital, though it is different, I did know about the routines, about wards, and the pecking order of doctors.' The most interesting thing he observed was a debriefing session for doctors and nurses after a terrible fire in which some children had died. 'It was really a counselling session for staff who had been helping the victims. People could say anything about how they had coped with it, or how they were going to cope. This was interesting because it reflected directly what *Casualty* is all about: the emotional impact rather than the medical detail.'

This was not something that Bowker used directly but it gave him insight into the feelings that an awful accident might generate, which he could then play out in the fictional *Casualty* department. He also thinks that speed is an essential element of the programme. 'Everything's got to be done on the hoof. If a member of the department took time out for a counselling session it would be noticed. Its advantage as a drama is that one can always get called away at a crucial moment. For a writer that's a gift. In my experience getting called away in the middle of an important conversation is closer to the frustrations of real life.'

A turnover of new writers is important for dramas such as *Casualty* which need a constant influx of new angles and fresh ideas. 'There's a ready-made structure to *Casualty* which could easily become formulaic; like a structure without a heart. It can become too pat: set up accident; emotional revelation; then out. You can get caught in that trap if you write too many episodes.' Oulton feels strongly that the BBC's policy of encouraging new writers on programmes such as *Casualty* and *EastEnders* is a healthy thing. 'That's the apprenticeship. I think you pick up good habits to do with structure and storytelling in a filmic way.'

Stories Bowker wrote for the 1987/88 series included one which sprang from a conversation with the mother of a girl he used to teach who was suffering from cerebral palsy. 'The mum was worried about how she would cope when Rebecca started to become an adolescent, have periods, want boyfriends.' He decided to write a story about what adolescent sexuality might be like for someone whose body has always been public property. 'People with cerebral palsy have an awful lot of tests, and have their body talked about in a fairly negative way. So what does that do to them?' He gave the story a happy ending. He made the boyfriend stay with the girl because he thought a positive rather than a negative ending would be nice for a change.

'I like writing for teenagers. Firstly because I think the teenagers in *Casualty* are usually really good for the storyline, and also because it's as if all the emotions are there that are in our adult lives but in a more vivid and surface way. Everything is felt in an extreme way, which can be liberating and refreshing. The advantage of writing for adolescents is that they tend to talk directly, so it doesn't come over as contrived. '

In another episode of series 12 he wrote about a rupture in an Anglo-Asian family between the older and younger generations. He particularly wanted to write something about family life and not about problems arising from being Asian. He thought that would be patronizing for a male, white, middle-class writer to attempt such an obvious thing. Also he was more inter-ested in what the areas of conflict are between the generations of a family from any racial origin.

A favourite story of his was about a love triangle. It involved a man hiding his bisexuality from the woman he was living with, while being stalked by his ex-lover. 'It was about the usual cesspit that goes on around relationships.'

Girls from a teenage roller-blading gang plot against each other in the series 12 episode 'An Eye for an Eye'. Emotions run high and sisterly rivalry culminates in a stabbing.

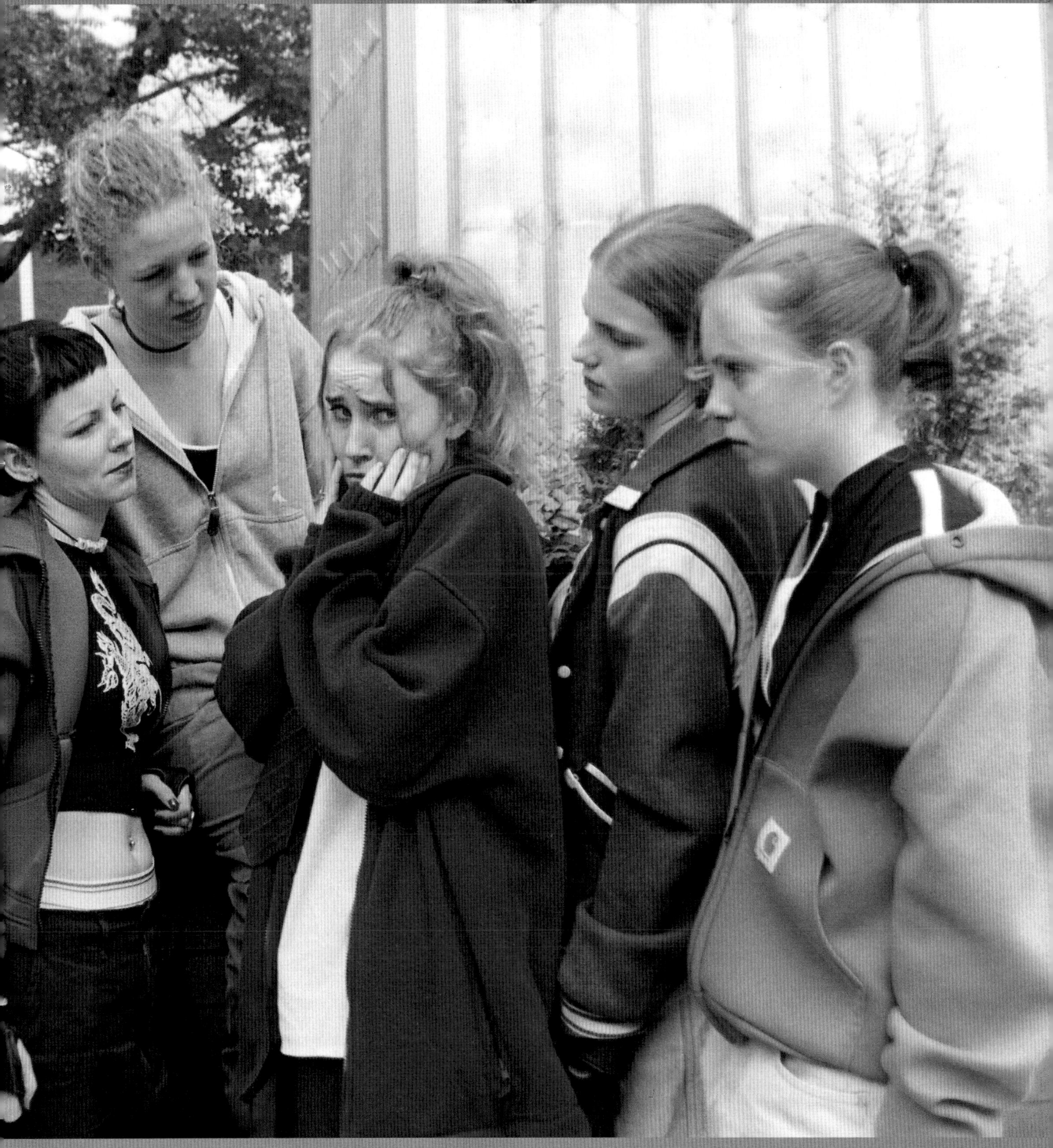

Bowker confesses gleefully, 'The nice thing about those sorts of stories is that you stick somebody on a hospital trolley so that they're trapped, and then they can't move because their neck is in a brace, and then just let their lives unravel in front of you. It's just bliss to do it, because it's everyone's fear: to be trapped while somebody walks in one door and somebody else walks in through another and they're the two people you just don't want to meet. Everyone, metaphorically at least, has been there. That's the fun of those stories – they can't control the situation any more!'

New *Casualty* writer and former actor Andy Rattenbury, originally from Dorset, went in search of inspiration one Friday night. He joined a paramedics' shift in Poole's West Dorset Hospital, arriving promptly at 7 p.m. to see the change in shift, and was immediately caught up in a dispute involving one of the drivers caught speeding by the police. They were determined to issue him with a ticket. A long argument was eventually resolved, and at last Rattenbury was able to put on the regulation green uniform and get into the back of the ambulance. In case anybody wondered what he was doing there, he resolved to say that he was a trainee.

'We got called out to an RTA – Road Traffic Accident – and I sat in a far corner of the ambulance. A man had smashed into the back of a parked car. When we got there it was clear he was paralytic. The paramedics got out and one had to make sure the drunk didn't do a runner. But he was too drunk to do a runner. The police arrived and wanted to speak to him, but the ambulance staff insisted on taking him back to Casualty to patch him up first. The police later took him off for questioning.

'There were lots of apparently mundane call-outs – a girl who had a dizzy fit, fights in a club. One very moving call-out was to an old guy who had fallen off his toilet. We went to find him. Then you're there in his house. He had been diagnosed with cancer of the bowel and his elderly wife was attempting to look after him at home. It's sad to be there at someone's moment of crisis. Frail and in his dressing-gown, it was not a front that he would normally have shown to strangers.'

This was one reason Rattenbury was particularly interested in going out with the paramedics: to see the beginning of the story. 'Once the patient gets to hospital they become more of a commodity.'

Later they drove up to the Control Centre, which in the Poole district is right up on the moors in one of a series of buildings which were used as a barracks in the last war.

Now abandoned, except for the one last hut at the top of the moor, it is a bleak spot. Dozens of startled rabbits were caught in the ambulance headlights as they wound their way up the narrow road. 'This HQ was staffed by five quick-thinking people who are trained to talk callers through a crisis. They try to keep people calm, while asking a series of crucial medical questions devised to ascertain the specific condition of the injured person. This information is then fed back to the paramedics as they are on their way to the scene.'

Staff at the Control Centre can also waste valuable time responding to the many hoax calls they get every day, and to vague messages such as: 'Someone's been stabbed outside the club...' Rattenbury's host ambulance was in fact summoned to deal with a man who had passed out behind one such club. The man turned out to be drunk rather than seriously ill, and the police were summoned in the hope and expectation that they would take him away to sleep it off in a cell. 'But the police were also reluctant to take him, arguing that the paramedics should take the responsibility. Basically neither service wanted to deal with a drunk man throwing up all over their vehicle.

'Then a woman phoned, alarmed that her child was vomiting up blood. When we got there it was clear that it was not blood. "It's Calpol, love," the busy paramedic assured the mother gently.

'I was out with the crew until nearly three o'clock in the morning. I left then because there was nothing happening and I was knackered! It is very tiring because of the stress you feel in the back of the ambulance. If the real paramedics had been as tense as I was, their necks would have been as hard as tables. But I learned that they are trained to be very calm, and used humour to deal with injured people such as a boy we encountered who had broken his leg badly at a youth club. They made him smile, putting him at his ease so that they could get him swiftly into splints, into the ambulance and off to A&E.'

Filming continues as experts ensure that an accident victim is given the correct early treatment to free his airway and allow him to breathe. The team at *Casualty* pride themselves on producing programmes that are medically accurate. A bonus for the writers is that *Casualty* has encouraged viewers to practise simple first aid.

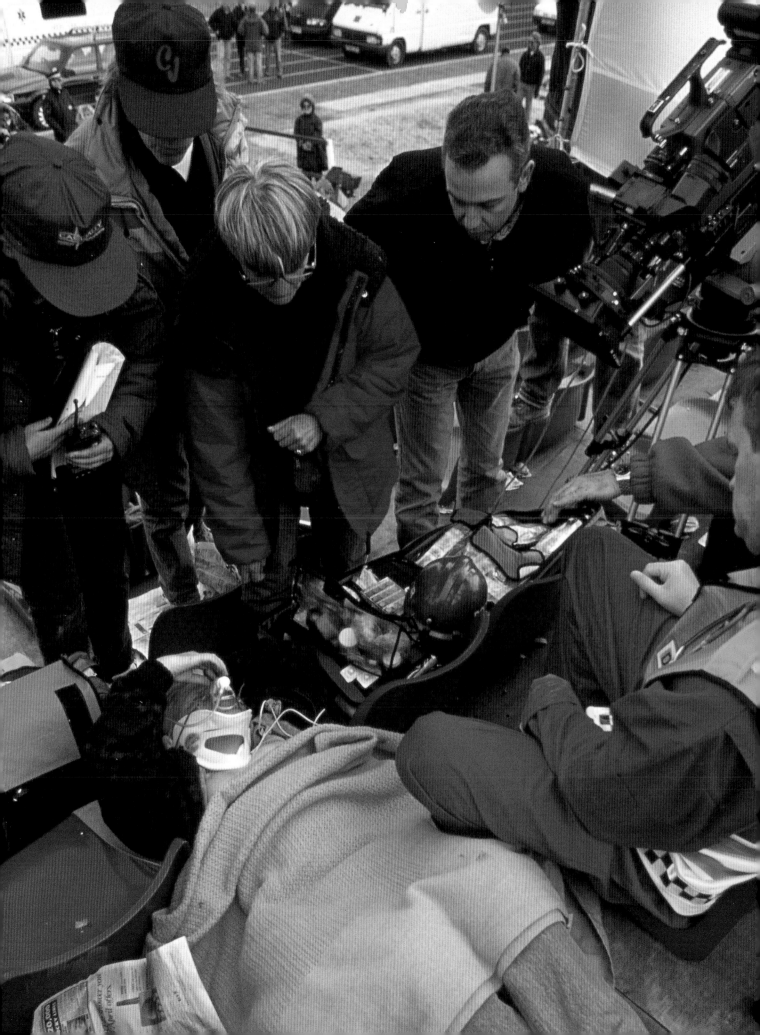

Trauma
CHAPTER THREE

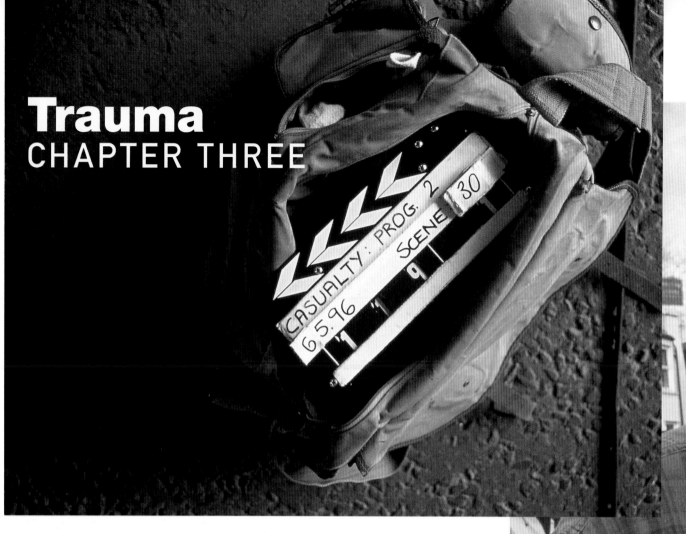

CASUALTY : PROG. 2   SCENE 30
65.96

The Production Itself

There is a screeching of tyres then an agonizing crash accompanied by that sickening sound of tearing metal and breaking glass. I jump back involuntarily. Standing beside series producer Johnathan Young on a grassy verge only a few metres from the road, which the relevant local authorities in Bristol had helpfully closed off for the morning, I suddenly feel as shaken as if I have witnessed a real accident.

'We're doing episode 3,' Young explains. 'Two people have just bungled the robbery of an off-licence. Yesterday we shot the sequence where they were coming out of the shop and the owner was whacking the front of the car with a baseball bat, smashing the window. So they're careering off course down here,' he points to a bend in the narrow road, 'and they collide with a man who is one of our other guest stories in the episode. A guy who was in the Falklands and wants to return a medal to the sister of someone who was killed out there. He's looking for her house down this street when these two robbers come

Casualty is always in a state of flux. Series 13 producer Johnathan Young amends a script while shooting episode 3 on location with his technical crew and stunt team.

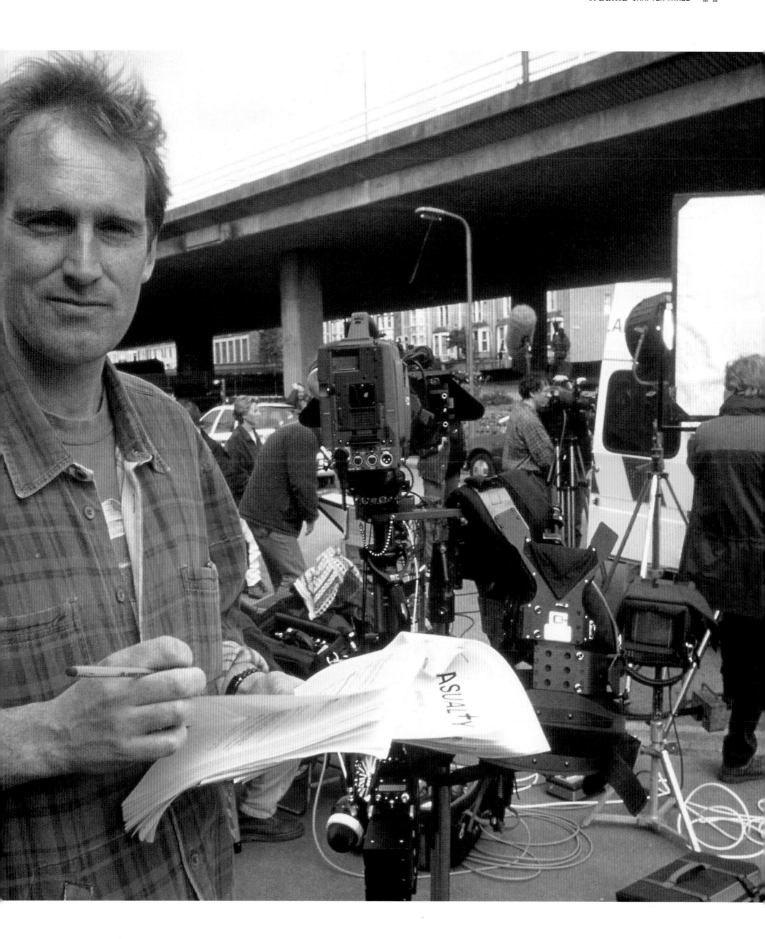

whizzing along, and knock him down before smashing into that parked car over there.'

Stunt co-ordinator Jim Dowdall has noticed my shock at the staged impact of the crash, and explains some of their safety precautions. 'We take the petrol tanks out so that the car is running on a tiny reinforced tank which only holds about two litres of fuel, and sits right at the back of the vehicle. That way, any fire risk is eliminated. Then the battery is tied down specially and locked in place. The driver is wearing a full harness and pads on his knees and legs. But in the end you are throwing two vehicles together at a considerable speed and there is kinetic energy and that is extremely dangerous. It is in fact the real thing.

'It's rather like fire in this business. A lot of the public have this misconception that we use cold fire, some kind of special effect where you can be on fire but it's not actually hot. Wrong: it is real fire. So when there is a guy on fire, he is burning. He may have protective equipment on and safety gels but there is only a very finite time in which he can be on fire.'

BELOW AND RIGHT Underneath his normal clothes a stuntman is extremely well padded to protect him during the filming of a spectacular (but carefully choreographed) car crash.

Four cameras are trained on the car crash and forty-odd people mill about: make-up, special effects, stunt men, actors, director and assistants, location managers and the technical crew. A table of light refreshments — tea, coffee and biscuits — stands rather forlornly in the cold blustery air, on the grey concrete area under an adjacent flyover. Despite the fact that it is May, the wind whistles through the concrete valley and I wish I was wearing the regulation fleece top and long padded windbreaker that practically everyone else is wrapped in.

Now huddled behind an enormous technical truck, Johnathan Young talks me through the process they have to follow before the stunt men can begin. They start of course with the script. Then they have to make editorial decisions about what they can afford, and what the writers want. The overall programme budget only runs to a certain number of action sequences which have to be paced throughout the series. At this stage the directors come on board and give a particular episode their own personalized vision. Then locations have to be found, before the stunt men and camera crew can even think about getting involved.

The stunt co-ordinator then discusses his concerns with the director. 'They'll look at the script together,' says Young. 'They will examine the feasibility of everything: they'll look at the safety of the stunt men, and the number they require; they'll discuss variables and options and what they'd really like ultimately to achieve. Then the associate producer, who deals with the finance, will get involved in the overall discussion about how easy the stunt is to realize. The production manager will be concerned with the schedule and how much time this particular element of the shoot will take.'

Each episode has to be shot in ten days, so the time taken to set up and shoot a stunt is a significant element in the overall time and cost calculations. Young expands: 'Ironically a lot of the simpler shots, like the point of view from inside the car, can often be the most time-consuming to film. Shooting something like this car crash with just two cameras, you would just run the car and it would take just ten minutes to do. But you need more camera cover than that. Sometimes that additional cover can have significant time implications. So all the discussions have to focus on all of these issues.'

Filming in England's notoriously wet climate poses its own particular problems for the camera crew.

Cameramen shoot from a crane to film the emergency services dousing a raging fire. Later on in the filming schedule the crane is used for shots of children being rescued from the burning building.

Today's car crash, he tells me, has taken half a day to film. 'On top of that we spent time yesterday filming the botched robbery, and the off-licence owner smashing the car window. Then add in the ambulance men coming along to pick up the pieces and the whole stunt component will probably take the best part of a day.'

The stunt co-ordinator explains further. 'There are two villains in the car,' says Jim Dowdall, who has thirty years' experience of such stunts and was responsible for the sophisticated stunts in the recent Bond film. 'They've both got masks on: one's got a rabbit head and one's got a cat's head. They're now in a panic, driving away screaming at each other because the robbery has gone wrong. They come flying round that corner where their car knocks over a man walking his dog. That throws them completely off course and directs them to what we in the trade call "T-bone a stationary vehicle" – which is one vehicle going into another at a ninety-degree angle.'

The stunt team come down to the location and 'recce' the site with the director beforehand. They discuss what exactly he wants the viewers to see and where and how he wants to shoot the action. They then work out at which points it is acceptable to use doubles and where they will have to use the real actors. As the robbers are wearing masks, in this instance, they can use doubles throughout this particular scene. Masks bought off-the-shelf would usually only have pin-prick eyeholes, but that would give a driver no peripheral vision. So the masks the stunt men use are made up specifically to their requirements, assuring the driver maximum visibility for accurate driving.

The dummy, although rather unconvincing in close-up, is perfectly realistic for long shots and is used here to represent an unfortunate victim of a sensational car crash.

Setting up the series 13 'spectacular': a truck driver is distracted by his mobile phone and swerves out of control crushing an emergency services vehicle. This sequence of images shows how much behind-the-scenes work goes into producing a convincing car crash on our screens.

'The stunt artists will be in the car doing all the driving throughout the scene,' continues Dowdall. 'We use another stunt artist double for the pedestrian who gets knocked over. We film the pedestrian as much as we can – walking his dog across the road as far as we can safely go, with the car just beginning to appear in the background. At the point when we are actually going to knock him over we substitute him with the stunt double. We knock the stunt double over, then we stop, go back, and set the whole thing up again. This time the car is going to crash, and "T-bone" into the other car. So it's the stunt double who is actually hit by the car, but now the viewers will see the actor lying on the ground.'

Compared to most programmes, *Casualty* has an enormous number of stunts and special effects. Dowdall worked on eleven of the episodes in the last series, including Barbara Machin's extravagant motorway pile-up in the Christmas special. He also did the big special effects for the opening episodes of the new 1998/99 series which involve a fire. 'In that script there were children in the fire, and obviously we could not put any children at risk. So we used a midget stunt double for the kids in a couple of the fire sequences where there was any risk. We then had shots of children coming through smoke, which was fine because we used totally non-carcinogenic, non-dangerous smoke. Then we cut to a sequence where there was a fire burning and mixed in separate shots of the children. In that way the eye is tricked into seeing them in the thick of it all.

'We also had a sequence where a child had been rescuing other children by finding a window at the top of a set of wall bars. He climbed up the set of wall bars and helped the others out of the window. But then finally he was overcome by the smoke and fell off the wall bars. In that case we set up a rostrum down below him with mattresses on it, so that he could actually start his fall. Then he drops away from camera, and we have the stunt double falling backwards on to an airbag placed over a crash-mat. When the children climbed up the wall bars they were all attached to a wire, with a wire operator at the top, so that if they slipped they would do nothing more than just hang there safely. In another sequence a child is lifted off the roof by a fireman on a cherry-picker and again, I used the midget.'

Dowdall attends regular health and safety courses to keep up to date. Despite his many years of experience, he still finds he picks up useful points particularly about fire procedures, and fire escapes which are very relevant to the work he is doing now. This is becoming *de rigueur* for stunt co-ordinators. But there are still accidents: 'You can't go against the forces of nature and gravity and expect people to be made of rubber,' he says. 'If you're knocking somebody over with a car, you can pad them up and they can be as experienced as they are, but they could land badly and twist an arm, an ankle or a shoulder. Those things happen. If you're setting somebody on fire, and the wind suddenly sweeps round you can have burns. If

somebody is falling off a high building, he may be falling on to a crash bag in relative safety; but then again with anything over forty feet you can never be sure that an airbag is going to be infallible. If you landed on your head, for instance, you would break your neck. So, in the course of a year people get injured, particularly if they're falling off horses and motorcycles or tumbling downstairs. You are going to get bruises if you hit the ground at thirty miles an hour, and it's going to hurt.'

The director and crew at work on location in the first episode of series 10, 'Family Values' in which a packed stand collapses at an athletics event.

Producers have traditionally come on from other programmes to produce *Casualty*. But Johnathan Young is the first producer to have also directed episodes of the series in the past and was even a production manager on series 5. 'The show has been going long enough now for people to come back in other guises,' explains Young as we speed back to the *Casualty* warehouse to join the cast at lunch. They will begin rehearsing medical scenes for episode 4, 'The Ties That Bind', later in the day. For writer Andy Rattenbury, it was a first *Casualty* script filming 'back-to-back' with episode 3.

'It's always supposed to be a big story every year that they're reinventing *Casualty*,' says Young. 'But I don't really believe that any producer has seriously gone in with the intention of "reinventing" the show, which is unnecessary because it's already very successful and works so very well.

'What we do find editorially, though, is that whenever a script starts to go a bit pear-shaped, we can go back to the very first treatment that Jeremy Brock and Paul Unwin did. They said then that *Casualty* represents the front-line where the doctors and nurses meet the real world, so you think, "Why is this current script going so wrong?" It's going wrong because that collision with reality is not happening in our script and it starts to fall apart. As long as you hang on to that basic premise the show will work. But I think that within that fine balance of serial element, medical detail, and personal and guest stories the show can be all sorts of things. It can be on location with the ambulances, or all in Charlie's flat, or Josh's house, or whatever you want it to be. It can be all those things when you earn it by sticking to those basic fundamentals.'

In charge of all aspects of the production on series 13, Johnathan Young pauses to give rushed instructions to a member of his production team back in the office.

As long as *Casualty* generally obeys those rules, an episode can break with tradition every now and again . For instance, Barbara Machin has written an episode which is entirely from Charlie's point of view.

Young admits that there is probably more medical detail in the first ten episodes of the new series than there was in the final ten of last year's series, but points out that there was plenty of medical detail in the first ten episodes last year. This change tends to derive from editorial decisions made about the personal relationships between the regulars, and about ongoing stories like the rape story involving Tina which ran over several episodes. 'We haven't got to that stage in our series yet,' says Young. 'What tends to happen first is that we have to give our new characters time to establish themselves; they have to be seen to be doctors and nurses. You can't launch into a big personal story involving them until you know them. As we and the audience get past the Christmas episodes, about- two thirds of the way through the series, and we approach the final third, the personal stories will develop.

'You try to build the regular characters,' he continues, 'setting up interesting dilemmas for them. You don't want to lose touch with the patients' stories, but inevitably after twenty-six or twenty-eight episodes people expect some sort of pay-off from us. So the serial element will grow.'

One new concept that Young has added to the ongoing production is a weekly collection of newspaper cuttings on medical matters, covering issues that are part and parcel of life working in the Health Service today. Collated by his script secretary and distributed to writers and artists, the idea is to get people thinking about the issues. Thus far it has proved popular and useful.

Ultimately Young regards his work on *Casualty* as being a little like the experience of someone who has inherited a stately home: he does not regard it as his, but something he has to look after and nurture and pass on to the next owner in a healthy state. 'I don't think that it is up to our series to muck around with the heritage that the programme has. I think you have to respect that heritage. The programme must move along, but that was always necessary. It was cutting-edge when it started, and it has to keep on being cutting-edge.'

Many people who work on *Casualty* have been there for twelve years, seeing hundreds of producers, direc- tors and writers come and go. 'You have to protect their investment and respect it,' says Young. 'Because that's why it's such a successful show. Apart from the fact that the basic format is so strong, it is the only reason we can do something this complicated. With even more

Cameras roll as Mike Barratt and his team battle to save a truck driver with severe burns caused by an illegal box of fireworks in his load. Medical advice is given for the filming of each patient who arrives in 'Crash' or 'Resus(citation)' so that all medical procedures are correct and no mistakes are made.

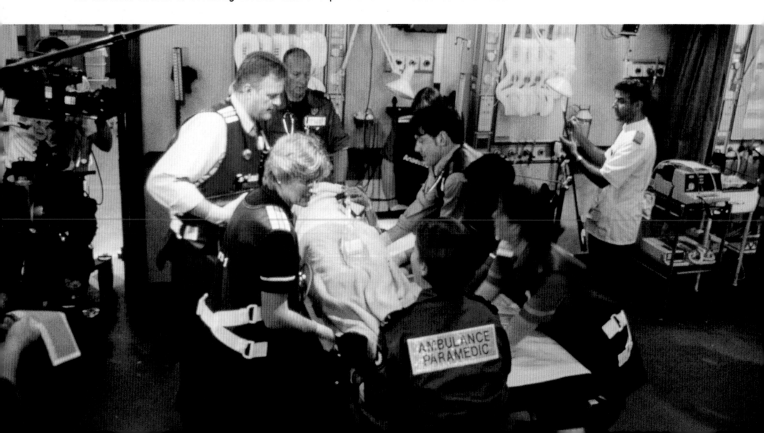

episodes this year, it's the biggest series ever and involves so much co-operation on the part of people in Bristol.'

The respect they get in Bristol, smoothing their way to such things as road closures, and their strong relationship with the medical advisers and hospitals in the area, is to a large extent based on the premise that the show is so believable. '*Casualty* has never been allowed to descend into melodrama or skew the research to suit. If the advisers say it absolutely couldn't happen, then we don't do it. I think that's why people think that it's real – because it is!'

In the vast *Casualty* warehouse Young gives me a rapid tour of the Holby City A&E set while the cast squeeze into a corner of 'Crash' for a group photograph. The department had been newly decorated

Ian Bleasdale and Sue Devaney discuss their next scene with the crew and medical advisers while an 'extra' waits comfortably on the ambulance trolley.

during last year's series, and Young had added to that a gleaming new lighting system, which would improve the look of the department and of the cast. Meanwhile the sound of the cast breaking into a spontaneous chorus of 'Food glorious food ...' between shots echoes cheerily through the set, as the photo shoot spills over into the lunch break.

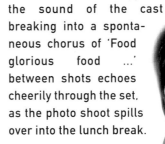

The *Casualty* set can be very disconcerting: 'victims' lie on on hospital beds with myriad different ailments, from asthma to broken limbs, while 'off-duty' nurses read the papers and drink endless cups of tea waiting for their big moment on camera.

Downstairs I see the familiar reception area looking spick and span: water is in the water dispenser, though it's not plugged in, and I notice that the magazines in the waiting area are up-to-date – unlike in many a waiting room. A children's cubicle has been added, decorated with ducks and clowns and the sort of nursery characters you might expect. There is a main entrance for the walking wounded and another round the back for the ambulance cases. Charlie's office is a small den within view of the reception desk, with the staff room and the formal relatives' room for breaking bad news at opposite ends of the ground floor.

Bounding up the stairs, we see new consultant Max's office, a shambles, as the poor man has only just moved in, and presumably has to deal with all the paperwork that Baz has neglected to clear up in the rush of her relocation to the new job in Birmingham. But this producer is not keen to see staff spending time in their offices in his series, preferring to keep them busy out and about interacting with patients.

With the fast-paced schedule of a show that runs weekly for more than six months of the year, and films from April to January with episodes overlapping, it is necessary to have a different director on each episode. Over the years director Michael Owen Morris, who is filming this day, has created something of a record, now on his twenty-fifth episode, but still maintains that every time he does it, it is a challenge and he sees something new.

'It's an aspect of life that, unless you're ill yourself, you don't actually see a lot of. Here with all the medical advisers you get to experience it from the other side. Though I think that there is probably only a finite number of medical stories that we can do, you can tell them several times from different angles and it's finding the slant on it that actually makes it fun.'

The director arrives four weeks before filming and is presented with a script, which is usually in a near-finished state, a third or fourth draft. He will then read it and study it, making notes, and then go back to the script editor and producer and ask to review particular areas, to: 'See if we can readdress any problems I spot and make a few changes so that we are all happy with

Michael Owen Morris, director of episode 4 of the new series, at work. ABOVE LEFT Discussing the shooting of an episode with the crew. LEFT Owen Morris goes over a scene with actress Barbara Marten, who plays Staff Nurse Eve Montgomery. RIGHT Owen Morris on location filming a mountain rescue attempt.

the end result,' says Morris of his own experience. 'They'll either agree or fight their own corner, but we come to an amicable understanding.'

While that process is going on, the director will be down in Bristol looking at possible locations, and casting with the casting director. It is an ongoing process with the different aspects all developing together. From there he will meet the technicians and go out to the locations and decide what to do where. 'I try and get home at that point,' says Morris, 'and actually sit down and do my preparation regarding shots. I write it all down and just read it and read it and read it, and become totally familiar with the script so that by the time I get down here the homework is done, and you can just relax and enjoy the shoot.'

The ease of preparation is very much dependent on the script. 'If it's a complicated medical story then we have to do the background work on it and find out where we're going with it. There are meetings with our

technical advisers to see how we approach a particular medical problem. Usually by the time I get the script most of that has already been sorted out. But, because I don't have first-hand knowledge of medicine, it's great to be able to come to somebody who does, and say, "Now how do you actually do this? And if I want to shoot it from there will I see what you're doing? Or can I avoid seeing what you're doing because I can't afford to see it in reality?"'

There was an occasion in the past, one of *Casualty*'s famous 'crash' scenes, in which a writer wrote three lines of stage directions. 'It just described that the man is ill, and they operate on him. I spoke to a medical adviser who said that the process he had written takes two and a half hours. Given that the show only runs for forty-nine minutes, I thought, well, how on earth am I going to shoot that? You have to find a way around it, like doing a montage of shots to compress the action, but still making it believable for an audience.'

A camera operator in hard hat confers with Michael Owen Morris during filming of the mountain rescue scene.

Owen Morris feels that the medical advisers have now got used to the show and realize that it is a drama and not a documentary, and understand that the team has to take a certain amount of dramatic licence. 'We don't want to offend them, and try and show the procedures in as accurate a way as we can, as far as we can go with that. It usually works very well.'

Episode 4 is now being rehearsed and filmed on the set while the episode 3 crew and director are out filming stunts – a 'double-bank' which can prove hard for the cast as they are rushing between the two episodes all the time.

It is also a complex task for the production managers, scheduling where the actors have to be every day.

The story Owen Morris is telling, 'The Ties That Bind', involves a girl coming off heroin, who has also had a miscarriage, having lost one of a set of twins. 'The problem for me here,' Morris says, 'is about dealing with areas that I've never experienced, and making sure that I get it right, and that the feel of it is right.'

Technically it has not been a very complicated episode for him. There are no major stunts, apart from crashing a couple of motorbikes. In the past he harks back to when he was involved with the famous episode where they burnt the whole hospital down, and he also directed the dramatic plane crash at Holby airport. 'Those episodes usually get banned as soon as I've done them!' he jokes. What he enjoys about the less stunt-heavy episode he is currently directing is that there is time to really concentrate on performances, and on telling the story.

Rehearsals continue on set, and I peek into the Aladdin's cave of the prosthetics room where hunks of unappetizing grey

Make-up designer Jill Conway builds up a silicone prosthetic chest piece (LEFT) and adds detailing and blood to the false body part with her assistant Liz Davies (RIGHT).

silicone, moulds for prosthetics, are stacked on shelves, and gory rubber body parts are spread across a large table. A prosthetics specialist on the set for a day sits patiently painting a small but nasty bloody gash on a hand. The gash gleams with sticky layers of reddish slime.

'After a certain amount of time working with these bloody body parts you become immune,' confides make-up designer Sue Kneebone, who has worked on *Casualty* since the second series. She now does about six episodes a year, which with two weeks of preparation and two weeks of filming she feels is plenty.

As a designer, she works out what needs to be made and commissions one of her two assistants to actually make the piece. 'Although I will apply a prosthetic and do the finishing touches, I am more of the overseer. I start with the script and then find out what the director actually wants to see. If he wants to see someone who has been beaten up, for example, then we start with natural make-up and through the progression of the story add swollen eyes after the fight, a different look if the character has to be resuscitated, or if he has a wound that needs stitching.'

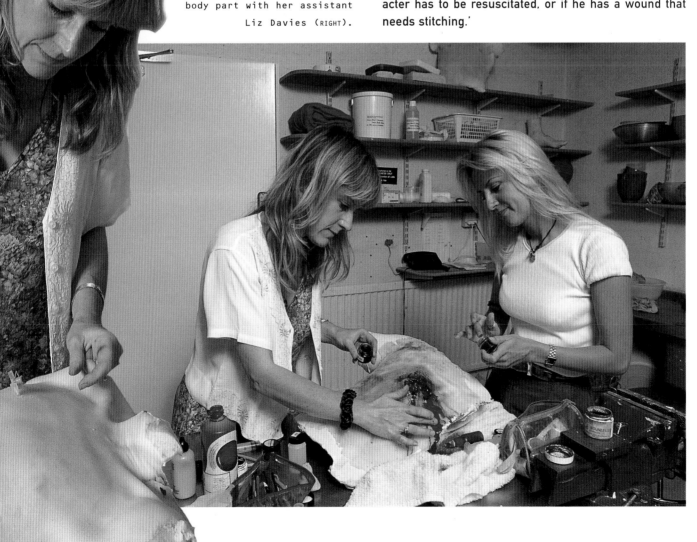

In episode 3 there is a character with a swollen eye, which is being made by prosthetics artist Marcus Whitney. Sue Kneebone explains that he would first take a cast of the actor's face in alginate, and then take a positive of that in plaster. On that he would make a moulding in wax or clay to create a swollen shape. 'Then he takes a negative of that, and with the positive and negative halves, once the wax is removed he would then have a two-part mould. Into this he would put a substance like fine translucent silicone or gelatine; gelatine could be actually painted in and would give you very fine edges, making it a very fine piece which would fit exactly into the actor's eye.'

When the piece has dried it is ready to be applied on to the actor using a prosthetic adhesive. Then the edges are blended away and colour effects added.

On the counter in front of us in one of *Casualty*'s two make-up rooms is what looks like a large circle of pink rubbery flesh with a gaping wound in the middle, showing torn flesh and bone. It is part of a leg which will be applied to a character who has been in a car accident. It is actually made out of a translucent silicone substance. 'There is no point in making the whole leg,' says Kneebone, 'if all you're seeing eventually is this little bit of femur. As a designer, my job entails knowing what will be seen and not being excessive in the making of something.'

In this case the character has been knocked off his bike by a car and has broken his femur. The prosthetic is simply

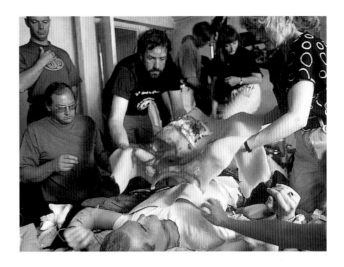

the bone that has torn through the skin and the trouser leg, and creates a nasty, gaping wound. The wound is smeared with a professional blood substitute called pro-blood. 'We tend to use blood that is syrup-based, so that it is quite thick and not free-flowing like water. It has quite a viscose, sticky feel to it, which comes off over everything and has to be constantly reapplied. No make-up is for ever, that's why we are here. What we try to do is keep the continuity and reapply over and over again. So if something is coming apart at the seams, or has been on since six o'clock in the morning and isn't used until eight o'clock at night, we are able to retouch and create what we had first thing in the morning.'

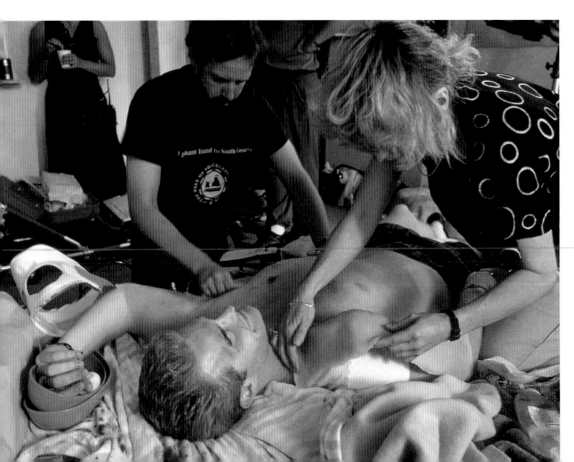

The make-up and prosthetics team apply a prosthetic piece over the chest of a hapless patient in series 9. When they have finished attaching it to his body he will be a major chest injury case in the episode called 'Crash'. Such moments will eventually keep viewers rooted to the screen.

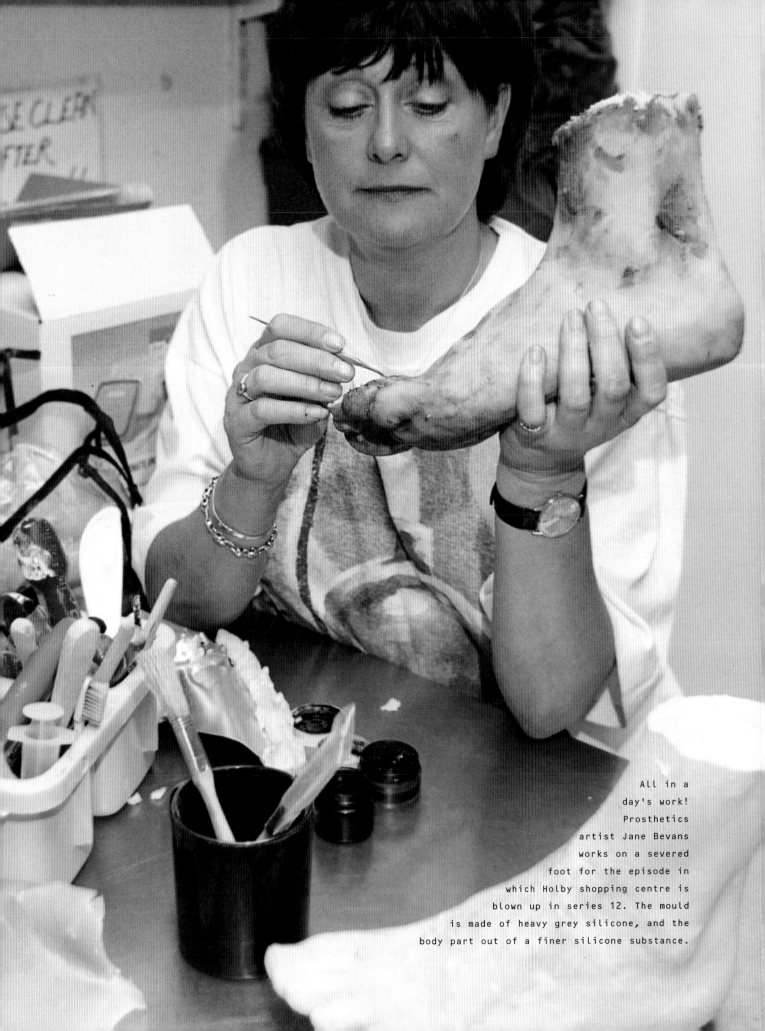

All in a day's work! Prosthetics artist Jane Bevans works on a severed foot for the episode in which Holby shopping centre is blown up in series 12. The mould is made of heavy grey silicone, and the body part out of a finer silicone substance.

Kneebone made up the track marks on the arms of the 'heroin addict' in episode 4 at eleven o'clock in the morning. She then found out that the actress was not actually filmed until four in the afternoon. 'In that space of time I'd applied the make-up three times because it had either come off, or – because she was also being handcuffed to a bed – the bed was rubbing against her skin so things were coming off.' The track marks were created by using a fine lilac wax, and then built up with blushing gels and wound fillers.

Sue and her two assistants make up on average twenty regular and guest artists per day, with an extra assistant who does all the supporting artists – which can amount to thirty or forty. Today they did fourteen actors first thing in the morning, and have been maintaining the make-up throughout the day. With other actors joining the cast at different stages of the day, the job can be a major juggling act but, maintains Sue Kneebone, 'This is one of the most organized sets ever. On *Casualty* we do have the time and the make-up to get it right.'

Here, instead of applying fake blood, the make-up artist gets a chance to make nurse Duffy look glamorous for a change during the filming of Baz and Charlie's wedding.

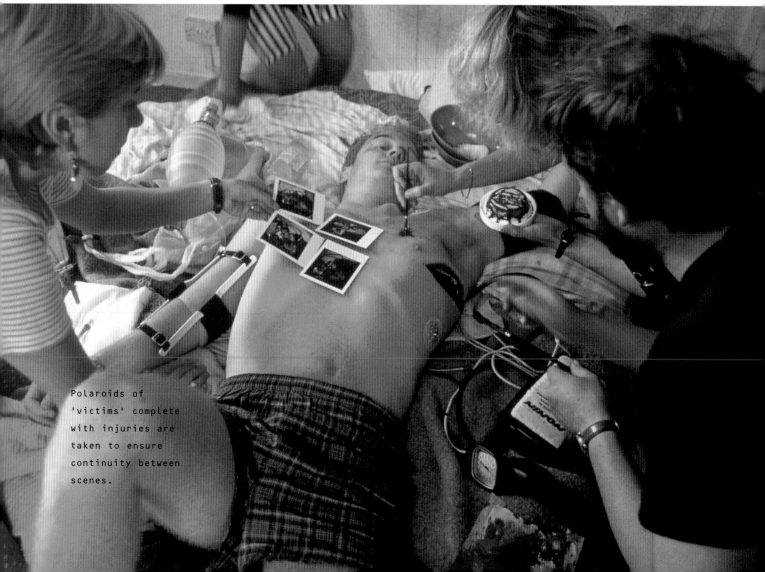

Polaroids of 'victims' complete with injuries are taken to ensure continuity between scenes.

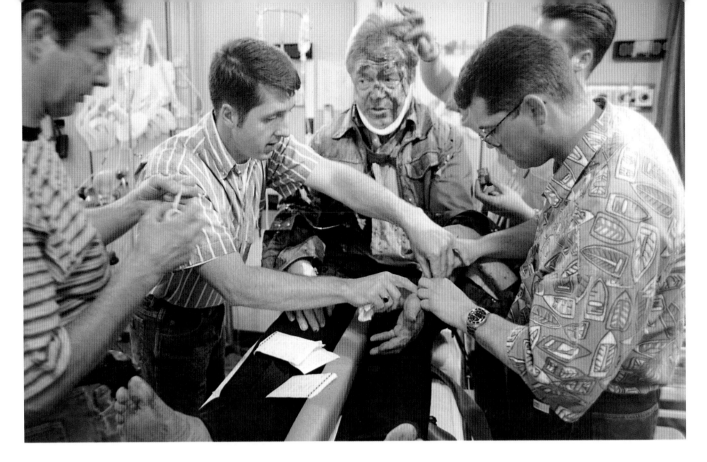

On set now, director Michael Owen Morris is rehearsing a scene where the regular cast are leaving the department at the end of their shift and heading off to a flat-warming party at Tina and Chloe's new home. The regulars are made up in what Kneebone explains is the English style – sparingly, using the actor's own features as a guide, enhancing some features and minimizing others. The Americans, she tells me, tend to go for a less subtle effect, and use make-up to cover the whole face and then build up what they want to see.

More make-up, blood and gore is applied to a victim of the Holby shopping centre disaster.

The regular cast are now out of their uniforms, and a new shift of extras in their uniforms are busily taking over in the background. Sam and Sunny lean against the reception counter, behind which Amy sits resplendent in a burgundy velvet smock. Duffy in a 'comfy' beige cardigan looks round the door of Charlie's office to see if he is coming with them, but he is too tired. Tina and Chloe argue when Chloe discovers that Tina has invited Eve. The raffish new SHO Sean inevitably walks out arm-in-arm with the girls. A camera rolls round the corner in front of me, and the second assistant, who is watching the proceedings on a monitor outside the door, cues in and directs the supporting cast of party-goers to make their way casually to the main exit.

Make-up artists maintain the many supporting artists playing accident victims throughout the lengthy shoot.

Diagnosis CHAPTER FOUR

A digest of the episodes that made up the **Casualty** story from autumn 1995 to spring 1998.

From the moment *Casualty* hit our screens in 1986, viewers have been glued to a mayhem of heart-stopping human suffering arriving at Holby City – plus the carryings-on of medical staff who treat the victims of accidents and self-inflicted injuries.

The casenotes of series 1–9 are summarized in *Casualty – The Inside Story*, published by BBC/Penguin. The storylines for series 10–12 begin overleaf.

From series 1 – which included a girl forced to drink milk after swallowing car fluid, and a man hit on the head by a golf ball – to the last episode of series 9, involving a seemingly innocent back-injury patient with an explosive device strapped to his body, demanding to know why his mother died at Holby, Saturday night's viewing has never been the same!

The trials, tribulations, love affairs and joys of the medical staff – from the introduction of doctors, Ewart and Baz, and nurses, Charlie, Clive, Megan and Duffy in the opening moments of the series, to other favourites, such as Kate, Ash, Jude, Mike and Josh – have proved as gripping as the people whose lives they battle to save.

The dynamics of the first and second series established *Casualty* as essential viewing, and, each time a series ends, fans hold their breath until the next begins.

The extraordinary success of *Casualty* is that we can believe that the dramas enacted on our screens could have happened to us or our loved ones. Thank God, we think, as we are roller-coastered through another nail-biting moment while a life is fought for, lost or won, that it is *not* us, *not* one of ours, but it could have been!

Series TEN: AUTUMN 1995 - SPRING 1996

Mike and Rachel attend the wounded when a poorly built athletics stand collapses, injuring among many others Jake, the builder's son; Duncan, an insecure fat boy whom Jake has been encouraging to try athletics; and Kelly, a young girl living with foster parents.

Duncan dies, and Jake has a badly injured leg – he may never be able to run again but, he tells his father, he will never join the family business. Baz diagnoses Kelly with severe spinal injuries. Kelly's real mother turns up at the hospital, but she decides to stay with her foster parents.

Baz is offered the post of Senior Registrar, but is unsure whether to take it. Meanwhile Charlie is feeling frustrated with their affair. Mike tells Rachel he is coming back to Holby permanently, but she is uninterested. In the middle of all this, new SHO Daniel Perryman starts at Holby A&E.

Horror as an athletics stand collapses.

EPISODE 1
Family Values
by LISA EVANS

When Mike Barratt and Rachel Longworth work together to help the injured, it is obvious that he still has feelings for her.

The crew prepare to start filming the collapse of the athletics stand.

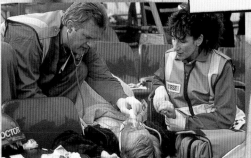

Josh and Liz arrive outside Holby City with the victim of an horrific farm accident.

EPISODE 2
Money for Nothing
by ROB GITTINS

Local farming inspector Pat Brown is trapped in a barn; he is saved, but not before one of the brothers who run the farm sets fire to the barn and is caught in the inferno.

An injured young surveyor informs Josh that he has AIDS. Staff become involved in his subsequent dilemma: should his life insurance policy be cashed now to support him and his wife through his illness, or used to support his wife after his death?

Daniel is accused of stealing a diamond ring, but it turns out that the woman owner has faked the theft to claim on the insurance. And Baz keeps Charlie on tenterhooks over her decision about the new job.

Sara Stockbridge plays a woman with money troubles who complains of having her diamond ring stolen. Daniel finds himself under suspicion for the theft.

Illegally adopted boy is kidnapped by a Romanian woman claiming to be his real mother. After an accident he is brought to Casualty where the truth begins to emerge.

Staff Nurse Kate's son is involved in a fire at an amusement arcade. He has been avoiding his irritable father, Trevor, who resents having been forced to take early retirement.

Liz is held at knifepoint by a clinically depressed man. Josh delays calling the police to try and talk to him. The man tries to molest Liz; she feels betrayed by Josh.

Charlie must make huge cuts in his budget. He also meets Baz's husband Peter for the first time. Peter tries to be friendly, though he knows Charlie and Baz had an affair nine years ago.

Billy, a clinically depressed man, is comforted by his mother. Forced to leave his beloved ferrets behind when he moves house, he holds paramedic Liz hostage at knifepoint.

EPISODE 3
Sacrifice
by KEITH TEMPLE

Animal-rights activists plant a bomb under a professor's car, but his young daughter gets into it. In rescuing her, one of the activists is injured and is taken to Casualty. Though he knows he will die, the activist refuses treatment derived from animal experimentation.

An ex-pat returned from Zimbabwe is thought to be suffering from malaria. But it transpires that, after a fishing trip, he has contracted Weil's disease from contaminated canal water, and he soon dies.

Kate sympathetically removes the wig that a man had glued on to his bald head. Laura, the new PR officer, shadows the nursing shift. On an adrenalin high, she asks Ash out for a drink after work which ends back at her place.

Police wrestle with animal-rights activist Wendy who is discovered at Holby City visiting her boyfriend who has been badly injured in the bomb blast.

EPISODE 4
Outside Bulawayo
by ASHLEY PHARAOH

EPISODE 5
Halfway House
by DAVID JOSS BUCKLEY

Following a gas explosion at a halfway house for the mentally ill, an injured resident dies in hospital. Daniel inadvertently brings together the mother of the victim and another resident, who caused the explosion. After a scuffle, the guilty resident runs off and throws himself under a train. He is rushed to Casualty but dies. Daniel is mortified.

Kate removes a fishbone from a man's throat. Still hoarse, he is discharged by Daniel. Mike abruptly tells Daniel to get the man back for a referral to ENT, the Ear, Nose and Throat hospital.

Charlie and Baz arrange an assignation after work, but both forget it is her wedding anniversary. Husband Peter turns up and invites Charlie to join them for a drink. Charlie does go to meet them, but cries off after seeing them together.

EPISODE 6
Compensation
by JOANNE MAGUIRE

A boy with cerebral palsy is brought in by his father, while his mother attends a hearing – she is suing the hospital where the child was born for negligence. The case is not upheld and she rushes to hospital; the parents are counselled on the best way to care for their son.

The mother's tense barrister is pregnant; annoyed when her boyfriend asks her to cut down her workload, she drives off and knocks down a woman on a zebra crossing. In hospital the couple sort out their priorities.

Rachel has a public argument with Mike, and later Charlie confides in her his own confused feelings about Baz. Even Ash and Laura are unsure of their feelings for each other.

After a frantic hunt, Josh and Liz finally rescue a stolen sick baby from a cold and inhospitable church.

A retiring detective constable finally comes clean about the illegal activities of his partner, who caused an accident in which the detective was badly injured and other lives put at risk. And a suicidal woman whose own baby died before it was christened steals a sick baby from the hospital; she takes the child to be christened, and Josh and Liz search frantically for the church.

Ash supports Jude's nomination for union shop steward. Charlie tells Baz he wants to finish their affair. For the rest of the night shift they avoid each other. But early next morning Baz turns up on his doorstep begging him to think again, and seductively leading him into the bedroom.

EPISODE 7
Turning Point
by TONY McHALE

A mother of two is in debt. One of her sons is beaten up, and she assumes it is her older boy, a 'bad lot'; in fact it is her well-behaved younger son who is in Casualty. He has been attacked by her creditors as a warning.

A Salvation Army officer falls in love again with a childhood sweetheart, now married and not a Salvationist. Distressed, he crashes his car; in hospital he says he will leave the Army. But the woman refuses to be the reason he abandons his faith.

An innocuous middle-aged secret cross-dresser falls downstairs and is taken to Casualty in women's clothes. Despite the tact of the hospital staff, the man's wife sees his stilettoes. Appalled, she blames herself.

EPISODE 8
Battling On
by ANN MARIE DI MAMBRO

Late one night, a five-year-old boy is brought in by Josh and Liz after a hit-and-run accident. It turns out that he had wet his bed, and his mother's new boyfriend had treated him severely. The mother tells her boyfriend to pack his bags.

A woman on 'acid' is brought in with a man after a car accident. Charlie suspects they were driving the hit-and-run car. But in fact the culprit is Stanmore, a senior doctor who has arrived with a cut head. He has a brain tumour and should not have been driving. And Baz is pressured when a man dies after being misdiagnosed by his GP and sent fifty miles to Holby because of the new fund-holding system. The man's wife threatens to sue.

EPISODE 9
Hit and Run
by BILLY HAMON

A mother with her son's favourite toy waits anxiously for him to come round after he is knocked down by a car.

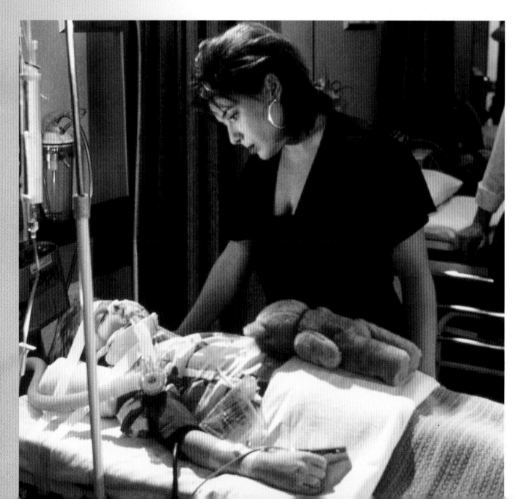

EPISODE 10
When All Else Fails
by TOM NEEDHAM

Baz is having trouble making up her mind between husband Peter and lover Charlie. As she ponders, she discovers that Charlie has grown tired of waiting and has arranged a date with another woman. Baz is left to mull over the mess she has made of her personal life.

Travellers Evie and Jim bring in their four-year-old daughter with a broken ankle. The mother is found to be in the advanced stages of breast cancer. She has endured it in silence as a 'punishment' for not giving up her daughter, borne as a surrogate for her sister.

Kate advises a young pregnant girl, whose jockey partner has just been kicked to death by a horse, to seek support from his parents. But they blame the girl for encouraging their son to carry on racing.

Baz has a dilemma with an elderly stroke victim, who has made a living will wishing to be left to die in peace. Active treatment has already been started, though; if this is negated, Baz feels it would be actively contributing to her death.

Called in to comfort a young patient's mother, a vicar tries his best to get out of officiating at a wedding ceremony later that day, but fails to find a replacement.

Mike tells Daniel that the hospital is being sued by the son of a Bengali woman wrongly diagnosed by Daniel. Meanwhile, workmen in the department upset the staff, particularly Rachel, with constant sexist comments.

After the wedding the best man, a gay liberationist, threatens to 'out' the vicar unless he owns up to his sexuality. Later the vicar hangs himself and is found by his housekeeper; he dies in hospital, and she confronts the best man, blaming him.

EPISODE 11
Release
by DAVID RICHARD FOX

On the river a boatyard owner causes an accident to his rival's pleasure cruiser, and a passenger falls overboard; both the owners are injured as well.

The passenger is an elderly man, attending a reunion of Holby City Football Club players that does not go smoothly. When the man falls overboard, another suffers a heart attack and dies in the rescue. Back in Casualty the survivors deal with their past.

Trevor Wilson, now security officer, has installed a new system that exasperates the staff. Laura and Ash argue about fund-raising events; Ash asks her out. Baz explains to Charlie why she is staying alone at a hotel; Peter wants to adopt a child as he is infertile. Charlie goes back to the hotel with her.

As Ash finally asks Laura out to dinner, *Casualty* audiences wait with bated breath: what does the future hold for this relationship?

EPISODE 12
Bringing It All Back Home
by ROB GITTINS

EPISODE 13
All's Fair
by KEITH TEMPLE

An amateur boxer throws a fight at his trainer's insistence, but collapses and is rushed to Casualty where he dies. The trainer blames the other boxer, who discovers what has happened and is devastated.

The agitated wife of an Army officer deliberately drives into a parked truck and is taken to Casualty. She tells Baz that she was an army nurse in the Gulf War; she believes she has Gulf War Syndrome, but the Army will not recognize it.

A student falls out of a second-floor window, having eaten a cake spiked with marijuana baked by his girlfriend. Baz berates the girl. Peter, Baz's husband, pays Charlie a visit.

In a schoolboys' gang fight, one of them falls down a steep incline and is taken to Casualty. The guilty boy tries to pin the blame on another, but their teacher finds out the truth.

Having had an operation, a salesman collapses in pain. In Casualty Mike discovers that he was not prescribed anti-coagulants after the operation, which might have prevented the blood clot. This does not augur well for SHO Daniel.

Ash agrees to go to the fund-raising ball with Laura. And Charlie and Baz eye each other warily.

EPISODE 14
Shame the Devil
by DAVID JOSS BUCKLEY

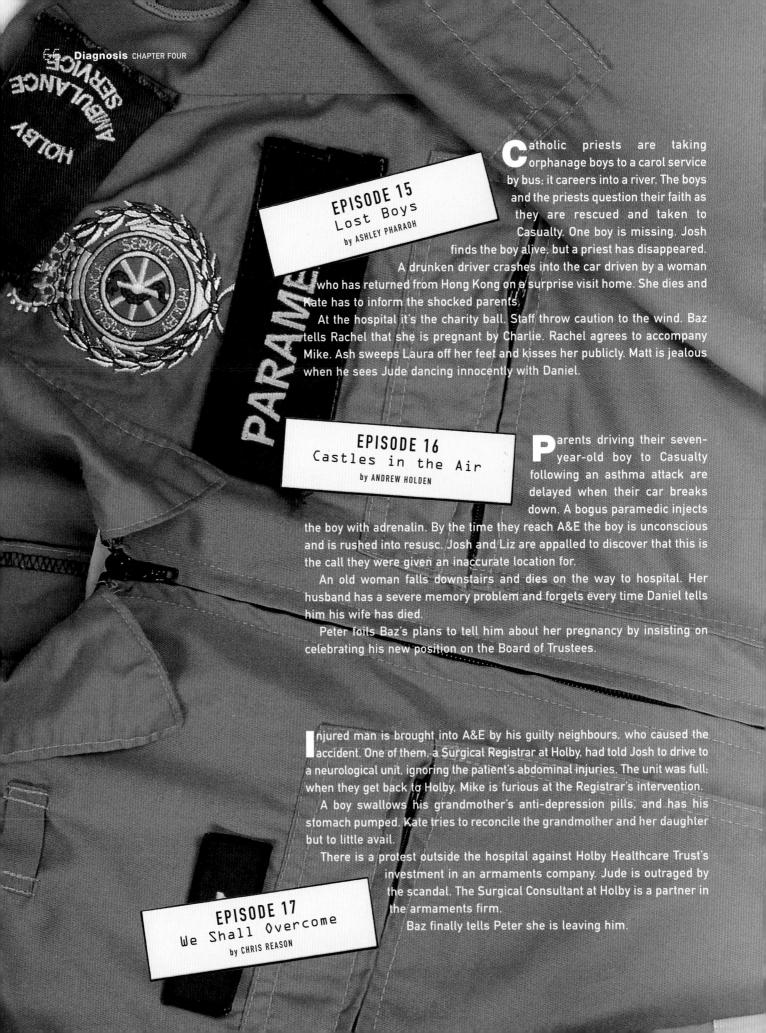

EPISODE 15
Lost Boys
by ASHLEY PHARAOH

Catholic priests are taking orphanage boys to a carol service by bus; it careers into a river. The boys and the priests question their faith as they are rescued and taken to Casualty. One boy is missing. Josh finds the boy alive, but a priest has disappeared.

A drunken driver crashes into the car driven by a woman who has returned from Hong Kong on a surprise visit home. She dies and Kate has to inform the shocked parents.

At the hospital it's the charity ball. Staff throw caution to the wind. Baz tells Rachel that she is pregnant by Charlie. Rachel agrees to accompany Mike. Ash sweeps Laura off her feet and kisses her publicly. Matt is jealous when he sees Jude dancing innocently with Daniel.

EPISODE 16
Castles in the Air
by ANDREW HOLDEN

Parents driving their seven-year-old boy to Casualty following an asthma attack are delayed when their car breaks down. A bogus paramedic injects the boy with adrenalin. By the time they reach A&E the boy is unconscious and is rushed into resusc. Josh and Liz are appalled to discover that this is the call they were given an inaccurate location for.

An old woman falls downstairs and dies on the way to hospital. Her husband has a severe memory problem and forgets every time Daniel tells him his wife has died.

Peter foils Baz's plans to tell him about her pregnancy by insisting on celebrating his new position on the Board of Trustees.

Injured man is brought into A&E by his guilty neighbours, who caused the accident. One of them, a Surgical Registrar at Holby, had told Josh to drive to a neurological unit, ignoring the patient's abdominal injuries. The unit was full; when they get back to Holby, Mike is furious at the Registrar's intervention.

A boy swallows his grandmother's anti-depression pills, and has his stomach pumped. Kate tries to reconcile the grandmother and her daughter but to little avail.

There is a protest outside the hospital against Holby Healthcare Trust's investment in an armaments company. Jude is outraged by the scandal. The Surgical Consultant at Holby is a partner in the armaments firm.

Baz finally tells Peter she is leaving him.

EPISODE 17
We Shall Overcome
by CHRIS REASON

An Asian boy attacks his sister for posing in pornographic magazines. She tells Baz and Ash that the money was for a recent abortion. She confronts her brother, and Ash throws him out.

A father supporting his daughter alone has a heart attack and is brought into resusc. He and the mother are finally reconciled. A man offers the department large sums of money, startling Kate; unfortunately he is deluded.

Baz tells Charlie she is pregnant. He wants to be involved, she needs to think. Laura faces a PR crisis when the press sniff out the trouble at Holby. She follows her principles and reveals the Surgical Consultant's huge mismanagement of hospital funds. Ash proudly asks her to marry him.

Laura is placed in a difficult situation as
the press demand answers from her about
mismanagement of hospital funds.

EPISODE 18
Land of Hope
by BILLY HAMON

EPISODE 19
For Your Own Good
by LISA EVANS

After attempting to escape from a security van, a kurdish asylum-seeker finds himself in Casualty. Jude tries to help him by contacting his lawyer, but he runs away and jumps to his death from the hospital roof.

Seventy-year-old twins who run a farm fight over the return of the son of one of them, adopted at birth. A shotgun goes off by mistake injuring one of the twins, and her sister drives to hospital. The childless sister has been jealous for years, lying to her twin that the child was dead.

Charlie tells Ash that Baz is pregnant, and Laura accepts Ash's proposal of marriage.

When a blind female traveller has an accident and is taken to Casualty, her husband tells Kate that diabetes caused his wife's loss of sight. Baz finds that she has cataracts, which are treatable.

A building worker gambles away all his money, and he and his wife are pursued by loan sharks. He is distracted on site and accidentally injures a colleague. The colleague dies and his wife leaves him.

Henry, the Surgical Registrar, confronts Laura over the Trust issues. But hospital management has decided to support him all the way. Mike is disgusted and decides to resign. He asks Rachel to go to Somalia with him. Peter confides in a reluctant-to-listen Charlie. Baz walks in and makes Charlie stay while she tells Peter of their affair and the pregnancy.

EPISODE 20
Asking for Miracles
by JOANNE MAGUIRE

EPISODE 21
Subject to Contract
by GILLIAN RICHMOND

A woman is in hospital to donate bone marrow to her baby. She argues with her jealous new lover, a woman, who has refused to tell the father of the child where she is. The mother runs out and is hit by a motorbike. She can no longer donate, so her lover must call in the ex-boyfriend, the only other potential donor.

A mentally disturbed young man is brought in by his mother; he threatens Kate with a knife, but is disarmed by Trevor. The mother is relieved when her son is at last diagnosed as a paranoid schizophrenic.

An initially hesitant Rachel decides she will join Mike in Somalia. They slip off after the shift, while the others celebrate the news of Ash and Laura's forthcoming marriage.

Persuaded by a friend to steal one last car, a young offender who wants to go 'straight' has an accident. His friend steals Charlie's car to go and rescue him. They both end up at Holby A&E, not badly hurt, but having to face the consequences.

A jealous fiancée asks a girl friend to spy on her intended at work.

EPISODE 22
Cheating Hearts
by ROB GITTINS

Not satisfied, she tries to run him down in her car, injuring only herself. At the hospital he breaks off the engagement. But he asks her friend out.

Although initially opposed to the idea, Ash's father agrees to come to the wedding. Laura is worried about her job, with Trust problems abounding. Daniel mis-diagnoses a patient yet again, which causes him to break down.

When attempting a vigilante attack on an allegedly violent youth, an elderly man has a heart attack. In hospital, the man feels enormous guilt when he learns that the youth was not the culprit.

EPISODE 23
The Way Lies Ruin
by KEITH TEMPLE

A businessman running away with his mistress falls down a stuck lift's shaft at the airport. At Holby wife and mistress meet. The wife leaves the mistress to face life with a man with spinal injuries.

Teenage girls with romantic illusions begin a fight over their handsome school bus driver, causing the inevitable accident.

Daniel returns after his breakdown and confesses that his heart isn't in the job. Charlie envies Ash's happiness with Laura and Ash advises him to go for it with Baz. Charlie duly asks Baz round to supper, and she accepts.

Two old comics, constantly arguing, are chauffeured by a woman around Holby nightclubs. At the same time, a sleepless man is out jogging and a woman in labour is being driven to hospital. And on the eve of Ash's wedding Holby staff, depleted by a flu epidemic, are working a long shift. During a lull, staff give Daniel a leaving present – he has found it all too stressful – but there is a call alerting them to a major RTA.

The chauffeur, distracted by her bickering passengers, swerves to avoid the jogger and crashes into the pregnant woman's car. Josh and Liz deliver the baby safely in transit. The chauffeur dies and the jogger's legs are crushed.

Trevor arrives to collect Kate to go to the wedding, but falls downstairs; the blow to his head sends him into a deep coma.

The wedding, when it is celebrated, is glorious.

EPISODE 24
Night Moves
by DAVID JOSS BUCKLEY

'Now you may kiss the bride.'

Holby staff celebrate Ash and Laura's marriage. Guest actors include Oscar James, Barbara Dettering, Valerie Hunkins, Celia Breckon and Richard Olley.

Holby staff watch as Mr and Mrs Ashton leave the church with bridesmaids Kirsty Fitzgerald and Georgina Edwards.

Series ELEVEN: AUTUMN 1996 - SPRING 1997

Baz has an emergency caesarean, Charlie arriving just in time to see his son born. Mike Barratt returns to Holby on a six-month contract; he deals with two lorry drivers whose load of illegal fireworks has exploded. One driver and a security guard die; the other driver is arrested. Kate's husband Trevor is now in a vegetative state.

A highly distressed woman is found wandering outside her car, her two children bound and gagged in the boot. Taken to hospital, she is admitted to a psychiatric ward.

Jude comforts a nervous woman who has lost a tampon inside her, and is worried that she may develop toxic shock syndrome. New SHO Richard McCaig has to extract the tampon.

Holby's happy family:
Baz, Charlie and baby Louis.

EPISODE 1
Chain Reaction
by ANDREW HOLDEN

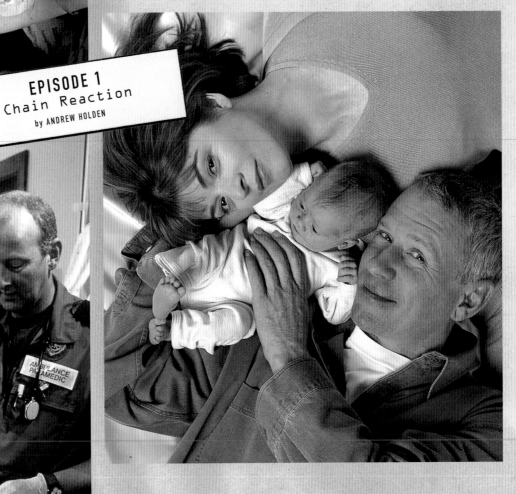

Team Leader

Josh brings one of the lorry drivers,
who is badly burnt, into the A&E department.

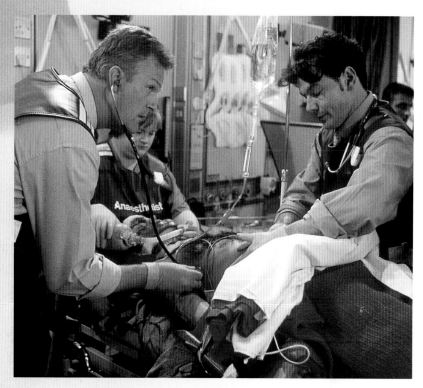

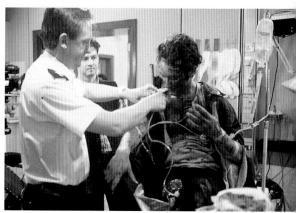

You're nicked — the second lorry driver is arrested for transporting the illegal fireworks which blew up his lorry and killed his fellow driver and an innocent security guard.

Doctors Mike Barratt and Richard McCaig struggle unsuccessfully to save the burnt lorry driver's life.

EPISODE 2
Relative Values
by CHRIS LANG

Twin sisters are brought into Casualty after a car crash. One has been having dialysis; both are now critical. When one twin becomes brain dead, her mother tells Mike that she would be a suitable kidney donor for her sister. Her father finds this hard to accept.

A twelve-year-old boy talks to Richard about a problem with his penis: schoolmates have been taunting him about its size, so he has been trying to stretch it, causing an infection. This trouble is linked to his anxiety about his parents' recent separation. Gloria, a nurse new to A&E, confronts the boy's mother.

Junior nurse Sam Colloby arrives for an interview. Unaccountably, Richard experiences numbness in his fingers, but is distracted from this problem by his warm relationship with Gloria.

Out on observation with the paramedics, Charlie is obliged to perform an emergency cricothyroidotomy — an operation to free the airway in an obstructed throat — by the roadside to one of the twin sisters involved in the RTA.

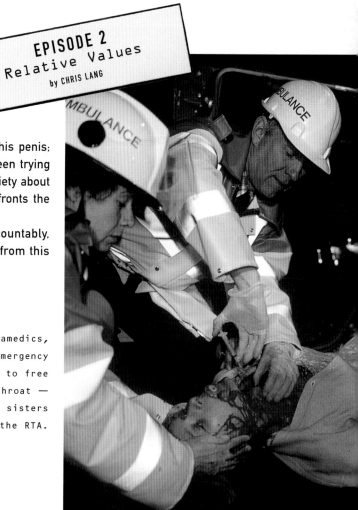

EPISODE 3
It Ain't Me Babe
by ROB GITTINS

Jude's ex-boyfriend Steve is brought in with a head injury, accompanied by his tearful young son. Jude discovers that Steve snatched the boy after his girlfriend left him for another man. Steve collapses, due to an underlying heart condition. Jude contacts his girlfriend who arrives as Steve dies. Both women are devastated. Gloria confronts Charlie on the issue of a new approach to bereavement counselling.

Mike and Charlie go out by helicopter to perform an emergency operation on a man who has fallen off a mountain ledge while trying to steal falcon eggs for his girlfriend to make money from. Sam consoles him back at Holby, his girlfriend having rejected him. Josh, scheduled for a place on the helicopter training scheme, is pleased with the success of this latest helicopter operation.

Mike Barratt must reinflate a young man's collapsed lung (caused by a fall from a mountain ledge) if he is to save the man's life.

EPISODE 4
Thicker Than Water
by KATE LOCK

Josh and Liz strive desperately to save a man's life after he is overwhelmed by toxic fumes from the chemical additives he is delivering to a swimming pool.

Two young Glaswegians come to Holby looking for their mother. The younger one is brought into Casualty when he is beaten up in a backroom gambling club, having found his mother there. She is a gambling addict, incapable of a relationship with her children. Nurse Sam, who has just won £200 playing pool, helps them with the fare back to Glasgow. His boyfriend, however, is disappointed to miss a celebration meal out.

An old lady slips out of her residential home and goes home to her flat. There she has an accident with decorating equipment. Without her knowledge, her husband has gone to live with another woman, renting out the flat. Devastated, she tells Jude she would like to sleep, but never wakes up.

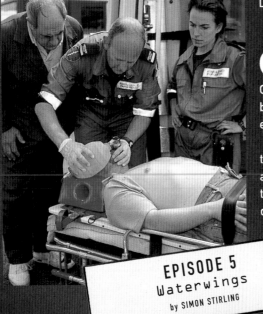

Chemical additives accidentally spill as they are delivered to a swimming pool, causing toxic fumes. Disabled swimmers are rushed to Casualty. A worker delivering the chemicals is also affected. Some students bounding around the department and annoying Charlie become much less ebullient as they witness the man's death.

Josh and Liz have a violent drug addict in their ambulance, picked up together with his more sensible brother and an unconscious tramp. Josh alerts the police as he searches for drugs. Back at Holby, staff suggest to the brother that he seek professional help to deal with the addict's drug problem.

Gloria's landlord turns up at Holby with her packed suitcases, advising her never to return. It turns out that she had once had a brief fling with him. Meanwhile, Richard experiences some problems with blurred vision.

EPISODE 5
Waterwings
by SIMON STIRLING

EPISODE 6
Still Waters
by MANJIT SINGH

Old man is chased by some young thugs to his allotment, where they find a grenade amongst the old man's war memorabilia. It explodes, causing one of the boys to lose his leg.

A junior lawyer arrives explaining that her boss made a pass at her and she reacted violently injuring him, having been sexually assualted in the past.

A teenage boy has eaten deathcap mushrooms; his horrified parents have to wait twenty-four hours for him to pull through.

Kate's daughter Lorna arrives, but disagrees with her about keeping Trevor alive in a vegetative state.

Sam offers advice to a sexually harassed woman who fought back, accidentally injuring her boss.

Josh and Liz rescue a girl involved in an accident in the middle of nowhere. Mike talks Josh through doing a chest drain over the telephone. Back in resusc. the girl deteriorates and dies.

EPISODE 7
Nightfall
by SIMON ASHDOWN

A baby boy suffering a neuro-degenerative disorder is brought in heavily tranquillized. Kate is suspicious at the amount of diazepam in his system. It turns out his sister has 'copied mum' and given him an extra dose to stop him crying. Believing that it is best to let the baby slip away painlessly, Kate finds a way of explaining the dose.

A father attacks the boy who supplied his daughter with the drugs she died taking. A car chase and RTA follow. Josh and Liz take them to hospital. Jude tries to calm the father, who breaks down.

Richard, Matt and Jude try to restrain the angry father of a dead girl.

A homeless drunk, well known to staff at A&E, is paralysed when she falls off a gurney and injures her spine. Her sister runs off, telling Charlie she cannot cope.

EPISODE 8
Vital Signs
by BARBARA MACHIN

A drunken, suicidally depressed RAF pilot is picked up by Josh and Liz. It turns out he has also taken an overdose of paracetamol, and even when his girlfriend arrives and he changes his mind, it is too late. The effects of the paracetamol overdose cannot be reversed.

While two grandmothers argue over the care of their grandson, he accidentally sets fire to himself. At hospital they are forced to come to terms with each other.

Richard's painful leg gives way and he is diagnosed with multiple sclerosis.

Amita Dhiri, more famously Milly from *This Life*, plays a mother whose son is injured when warring grandmothers do not notice his plight.

Dr Richard McCaig has to admit that he has medical problems of his own. After he takes a tumble in A&E, he protests to Jude that the place is too cluttered. But the reality is that his condition is far more serious.

EPISODE 9
Another Day in Paradise
by TONY McHALE

Two little girls are rescued by Josh and Liz in the helicopter from a caravan site where a caravan has come adrift and crashed. Parents argue about whose fault it was. One of the mothers has to reconsider how she has brought up her child.

A young builder is brought in with an arm wound caused by a chisel. It transpires he has a history of self-mutilation. He leaves after being stitched up, but is later rushed back into Holby having jumped off a high-rise building.

Trevor has pneumonia, and Kate and her children must decide whether he should be treated or not. With anguish they decide not to allow treatment. On Baz's first day back the nanny brings baby Louis in to visit.

Josh and Liz use a different type of vehicle to their trusty ambulance, performing a daring helicopter rescue of two little girls from a caravan site.

EPISODE 10
Bad Blood
by LILIE FERRARI

A bloodied woman walks into Casualty in her nightie, unable to remember anything. A man is wheeled into resusc., having fallen off a ladder. The amnesiac woman is his wife. He has been looking after her himself but clearly cannot cope.

A teenage girl has terrible abdominal pains. When she is rushed into hospital her parents are sure she is having an abortion, but in fact she has a build-up of menstrual blood due to a sealed hymen. As the parents argue the girl slips out of Casualty.

Trevor dies and, alone with his body, Kate wonders whether she did the right thing. She watches the other staff going off to Mike's surprise leaving party. Richard and Gloria get drunk and leave early together, as do Matt and Jude.

Kate and Trevor in happier times. In this episode we say goodbye to former hospital security officer, Trevor Wilson.

Charlie breaks the news of their friend's death to two elderly ladies (played by Phyllis Calvert and Anna Wing). Luckily they believe in reincarnation.

Refusing to move to a retirement home, an old lady barricades herself into her room. She suffers a stroke and two friends accompany her in Josh's ambulance to hospital, where she dies. A heavily pregnant woman brings her injured father into Casualty and suddenly goes into labour; she gives birth to a boy. The old ladies are thrilled – their friend always said she would come back as a man. This amuses Gloria; she and Richard are getting on rather well since Mike's party.

Jude and Matt, however, are feeling awkward. Jude looks after a suspiciously young girl brought in by an unidentified man who leaves her with £50. New Consultant Jack Hathaway asks her if the man is her pimp. Outraged, the girl explains that he is her employer at a factory but she is under sixteen.

EPISODE 11
Made in Britain
by LISA EVANS

Finding her mother in a drug-induced stupor, a young girl seeks a neighbour's help to phone the doctor, but is attacked by a guard dog. The neighbour calls an ambulance. In Casualty Sam finds out that the young girl is pregnant. She is brought in but loses the baby.

It upsets Baz to tell the woman that her baby died; she talks to Charlie about reducing her hours to spend more time with Louis. A bridegroom who collapses at the altar with an epileptic fit is married to his bride in a Casualty cubicle. Gloria deals with an infected pierced belly button. The boy refuses to have the ring removed as it was part of a bet. Richard saves the day by taking a Polaroid as proof. Gloria accepts an offer of a drink from Richard.

EPISODE 12
Mother's Little Helper
by PETER MILLS

A woman is pulled out of the river, bound and gagged. She tells Jack she has swallowed a package of heroin. It turns out that the investigating officer who arrives at Holby is the man who threw her in. With evidence from the camera in the resusc. room Sam manages to prove that he is a drug trafficker.

A Care in the Community couple skid off the road on their motor bike. The boy hurts his leg and his girlfriend attempts to leave him until Matt persuades her to stay. Meanwhile Jude discovers that she is pregnant, despite using a condom.

Gloria's ex-boyfriend comes in to see her, registering as a patient to force her to speak to him. He is abusive to her. Richard overhears, and sees him off the premises.

EPISODE 13
Trapped
by ANDREW HOLDEN

A busy time for Jude who here reassures an
injured motorbike enthusiast and in the same
episode discovers that she is pregnant by Matt.

Matt intervenes when a cleric attacks the drunken driver who mowed down his sister and niece. The cleric explains that his distress is made worse by the awareness that he has a public role to fill.

A six-year-old girl, distressed when told that Father Christmas does not exist, runs into the garden, smack into the greenhouse. Staff are amazed at her father's insensitivity, and Jude asks Matt to arrange for the Santa from a children's ward party to visit her. Santa duly pops his head round the girl's curtain, and she drifts off into a happy sleep. Jude thanks Matt. But he is perplexed; he was unable to arrange the visit as the ward Santa was off with flu.

Jude tries to tell Matt she is pregnant, but then changes her mind when she hears he has been asked to run a bar in Crete.

EPISODE 14
Do You Believe in Fairies?
by DEBORAH COOK

Could this be the real Santa Claus?

EPISODE 15
The Dying of the Light
by CHRISTOPHER REASON

Jude, preoccupied with her pregnancy, is not sure if she will make it to the staff Christmas party. A singer is rushed into Casualty suffering from an epiglottic abscess and will need surgery: she cannot take part in a Christmas show and her director cancels it. But Matt, overhearing, books the company for the party.

A stroke victim brought in for respite care has another stroke and falls downstairs. Jack allows him to die in resusc., as the humane course. The patient's wife and son are with him when he dies and the experience brings them closer together.

At the party Jude tells Matt her news; while Matt catches his breath, she storms off. Gloria and Richard enjoy the party: they are going away for Christmas together. Kate looks stunning, but her brave façade soon crumbles. Matt finds Jude and assures her of his support. Meanwhile, the music company lead a naughty singalong.

Dressed to kill — *Casualty* staff celebrate Christmas with a James Bond-themed party.

EPISODE 16
The Homecoming
by CHRIS LANG

Paroled after fifteen years, a sex offender is *en route* to his mother. His victim's parents live nearby and, together with local vigilantes, have mixed reactions. The victim's father ends up in A&E when he clashes with the vigilantes, as does the offender who is beaten up. In a cubicle the remorseful offender asks the father to smother him; but though he wants to do it he cannot.

Jack attempts to save the life and unborn child of a heart attack victim, wife of a skinhead also just released from prison. But the woman dies, leaving her husband with nothing. Jude decides to have an abortion, and Matt offers to go with her. Gloria discovers that Richard has MS; he explains he did not tell her as he does not want pity.

While a mother watches her boyfriend scuba diving, her little boy falls into the water. The child is airlifted back to Holby; his mother wonders whether her desire for a relationship has endangered her son.

Liz and Penny, in the ambulance, are called out to a baby who turns out to be baby Louis who is being looked after by his nanny, Margaret. Back in A&E Baz is traumatized when she has to take a blood sample from her own baby. But it is only a febrile convulsion due to overheating.

A suspected meningitis case turns out to be food poisoning. A man and a woman are brought in. He has hit her over the head in an attempt to stop her fellating him while in the middle of a seizure.

EPISODE 17
Hidden Depths
by SIMON STIRLING

Aileen, a difficult patient, takes out her frustrations on an overworked Charlie, who is also distracted when the nanny Margaret brings Louis in, having found blood in his nappy.

EPISODE 18
Tall Tales
by DAVID JOSS BUCKLEY

Josh and Liz arrive with a man suffering chest pains, but with no symptoms. He explains the pains are those of his twin brother, who indeed turns up having a heart attack and dies. The other twin's pain stops abruptly, but then he suddenly drops dead.

Louis is found to be in perfect health, but the nanny then tries to smother him. A psychiatrist suspects Margaret has Munchausen's Syndrome.

Charlie has accidentally brushed against Aileen, who accuses him of sexual harassment and makes an official complaint.

Is baby Louis in safe hands? Nanny Margaret is found to be dangerously out of control.

EPISODE 19
Déjà Vu
by LILIE FERRARI

When a mother-of-four discovers her sister is pregnant by her prisoner husband, she rams her car into the van taking her husband to a court hearing. The husband and other prisoners get out, and the injured are taken to Holby. When her husband thanks the woman for helping him escape, she explains that she was actually trying to kill him.

A journalist checks in as a patient, hoping to get a story on Charlie, who is facing sexual harassment charges. Baz soon puts him in his place, and he opts to cover the escaping prisoners story. All the staff (except Jude and Matt who are at an abortion clinic) are interviewed about Charlie; Richard is so irritated he storms out.

EPISODE 20
Treasure
by LISA EVANS

A man who does odd jobs for neighbours is digging a well when it collapses in on him. When his wife takes him to Casualty she discovers he is not, as she thought, cheating on her with another woman, but cheating the other woman by selling her paintings for a huge profit. A woman chats to a man in Reception while they wait to be seen. She manages to diagnose his condition as something she saw on *Flying Doctors*.

Josh and Liz get an emergency call out to a fire at Josh's address. His wife and son die, and they rush his daughter to A&E. Staff battle to save her, but fail. Josh is poleaxed.

Neighbours watch as a local house goes up in flames. Tragically it is the house of paramedic Josh.

A fireman restrains Josh as he desperately attempts to rescue his family.

Paramedics do all they can but they cannot save Josh's wife and child.

EPISODE 21
United...by Blood
by TONY McHALE

Two feuding extended families appear *en masse* in Casualty with a variety of injuries. They continue fighting until a chase ensues and the son of one family is pushed off the first-floor balcony. This shock sobers them all.

A boy is brought in with a broken collar bone, and Richard suspects abuse. It turns out not to be so; the boy fell downstairs after walking in on his father and uncle 'together'.

It is only a week since Josh lost his family; he is off work, but comes in to ask Baz how much pain they would have suffered. She tries to comfort him. Matt announces he is off to Crete, telling Jude he is only going because he felt there was nothing left for him here after the abortion.

EPISODE 22
Make Believe
by KATE LOCK

A haemophiliac is treated after a knife attack. He is puzzled when Kate tells him a friend told them about the haemophilia. The friend enlightens him: she works for the same company and had read his personal file as she had a crush on him but was too shy to speak to him. He forgives her and asks her out.

The staff celebrate Matt's move to Crete in a local pub. There Matt and Sam find their opponents at pool poor losers and after a punch-up they and other members of the staff end up back at Holby, this time as patients rather than doctors and nurses.

Dominique, a glamorous South American medical student who did some training with Richard, is observing in the department. Gloria is rather jealous. Dominique is okay until she sees a child die of meningitis. She rushes off, and Gloria finds blood in the basin. Dominique has been relieving stress by draining her own blood; she admits to Richard that the pressure is too great for her. Bereaved Josh is back on the job with Liz, but she is unsure he is ready. Matt and Jude say goodbye.

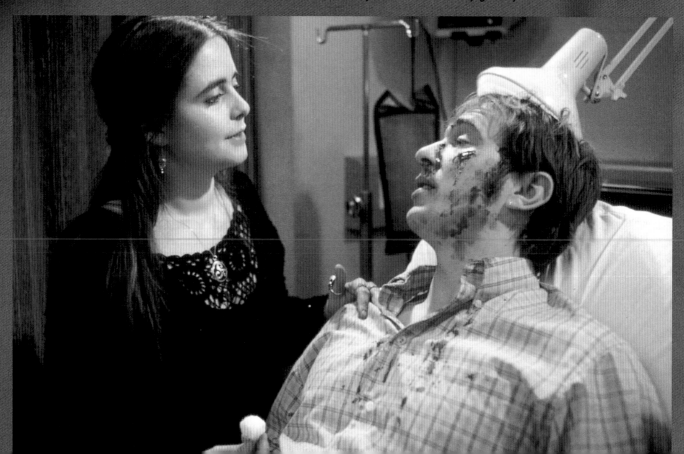

EPISODE 23
Monday Bloody Monday
by BARBARA MACHIN

Charlie deals with the frustrating problem of insufficient numbers of beds at Holby as he tries to find space for a distressed Care in the Community psychiatric patient.

The under-strength staff must cope as best they can. An elderly woman collapses in the car park; she explains her distress that an old lady friend has a potentially malignant mole. Josh and Liz are later called out to the same woman who dies of an aortic aneurysm.

Kate presses a panic button when confronted with a violent drunk. Jack is stood up by his girlfriend. Gloria is upset to find that Richard has applied for an anaesthetist's post elsewhere. Jude is the only overworked member of staff in a good mood, as she has had a letter from Matt.

A porter suddenly reports that a nurse has collapsed in the corridor. No one is prepared for it to be Jude, and that she has been stabbed.

EPISODE 24
Perfect Blue
by BARBARA MACHIN

Jude is rushed into resusc., where Jack discovers she has been critically injured. Police arrive to investigate. Matt phones from Crete and is told of the attack; he gets on the first flight. Baz and Kate are surprised to learn how close the two are.

Shocked by Jude's stabbing, Josh is extremely shaky when called out to a man with a clot in his leg. He loses his temper and Liz later confronts him, saying she thinks he needs counselling. Josh breaks down.

Matt has arrived in a terrible state. Police discover that Jude was stabbed by a heroin addict with a psychiatric record. Matt sits by Jude's bed in intensive care.

In the final episode of series 11, Jude lies close to death after being stabbed. As colleagues struggle to save her life and police try to find her attacker, an auguished Matt keeps vigil.

Series TWELVE: AUTUMNN 1997 - SPRING 1998

EPISODE 1
Give My Love To Esme
by GINNIE HOLE

Baz and baby Louis are caught up in a bomb explosion in a shopping centre. Fortunately they escape, and Baz helps the emergency services. The injured include a youth whose baby son was delivered to his seventeen-year-old girlfriend Esme in Josh's ambulance that same morning; a couple in their sixties buying gifts for grandchildren they are to visit for the first time in Australia; and a couple in their twenties who argue because the girl wants to join the police force.

Tension runs high in Casualty as the many injured are brought in. It is especially hard for Charlie until he discovers that Baz and Louis are safe. Staff Nurse Kate Wilson is delighted to announce that Matt and Jude have married in Crete.

ABOVE Emergency services rush to a shopping centre in Holby following a devastating explosion.

Baz is forced to amputate the leg of a teenage father in order to free him from beneath a concrete pillar in the devastated shopping centre.

A teenage girl is badly beaten up; Casualty staff quickly identify her as a prostitute and warn her of the dangers. But even when she finds out that it was her friend who arranged for her to be beaten up, in order to keep her on the game through fear, she discharges herself from hospital and goes back to her 'family'.

A woman is brought in after falling downstairs; Kate and Richard discover other injuries and, when her grown-up son loses his temper in the plaster room, staff begin to realize what has been going on.

A pensioner is brought in by her young neighbour with lacerations to her arm. Sam discovers that the two have been fighting about a boundary fence; he suggests to the younger woman that perhaps her neighbour is lonely and the matter could be resolved over tea and scones. The neighbours are reconciled.

George suspects that a badly beaten girl has been working as a prostitute.

EPISODE 2
Private Lives
by ROBIN MUKHERJEE

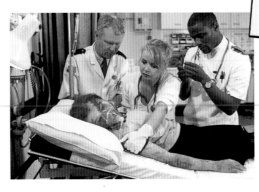

RIGHT Tina wonders whether General Manager Elliot is doing enough to ensure the personal security of staff.

Aman about to leave his wife is delayed when she deliberately hurts herself and he has to bring her to Casualty. It turns out that he has made his money importing drugs and is now attempting to escape business rivals. He fails to escape: a motorbike rider enters the hospital and shoots him dead. General Manager Elliot then faces demands for improved security.

A teenage boy is brought into A&E after drinking too much vodka. Kate discovers that his mother, like herself, has recently been widowed. The boy is drinking because he thinks his mother blames him for his father's death. Kate helps the two to talk and think about the future.

Tina is reprimanded by Charlie when she deals sharply with a difficult old man, a first aid 'expert' who has insisted on telling the medics how to do their job.

Kate has money problems and her anxiety spills over into work. Richard and George clash over patients, and Jack advises Richard to take it easy because of his MS.

Teenager Zeph, in with a slashed face, boasts of gang violence in Holby. When his grandmother turns up, it emerges that Zeph's real name is Godfrey and he isn't as streetwise as he pretends.

A young couple are at their wits' end with their crying baby. They fight and the woman is injured. At hospital it comes out that they have been attacking each other for some time and the relationship is at an end.

Instead of looking after her friend's young son, a woman scores some 'smack', and the boy is knocked over by a cyclist. The boy survives but the friendship is sorely tested.

Feeling ill and not wishing to tell anyone about his MS, Richard stands George up for a promised drink. Mark happily takes his place.

Money is available for the department, but it is to be spent on refurbishment rather than on security equipment. Elliot faces trouble.

A teenage girl with cerebral palsy is brought in by her new boyfriend following an epileptic fit. She has stopped taking her medication as an act of rebellion, but is encouraged to come to terms with her body and her budding love life by Mark and George. These two are themselves in a quandary, having spent the night together. Richard is still interested in George, and is perplexed when she rebuffs him.

Two sides of a family are locked in a dispute, which culminates in a reckless car chase and horrific crash. It is only in hospital when the mother dies that they are able to work out their differences.

Baz misses Charlie who is away on a course. Mark and George kiss and make up.

Mark and Josh separate clashing rollerblade hockey players.

Eddie (on the right, played by Ray Emmett Brown) accuses Darren (Ramon Tikaram) of losing them the game due to his age and lack of speed.

An overworked boy of thirteen is injured in a rag trade sweatshop. He is an illegal employee, and other staff call the paramedics when the boss is reluctant.

An argument breaks out between rival members of the same rollerblade hockey team; they attack each other and are both injured. Mark and Sam are forced to pull them apart.

Liz's boyfriend leaves her for another woman, and she apologizes to Josh for her recent bad temper. An elderly woman brings in her 'sleeping' husband. Kate breaks the news that he is dead, but it is some time before the woman can accept this.

Tina calls Social Services about the injured sweatshop boy, and regrets it when his desperate mother appears.

EPISODE 6
Counting the Cost
by TONY McHALE

EPISODE 7
Always on My Mind
by SHELAGH STEPHENSON

Kate is feeling the strain of her secret addiction to shopping; she tells Baz she is thinking of leaving. Sam is irritated by his out-of-work boyfriend.

Jack decides not to attempt resuscitation of a woman in her seventies who is brought in by her sister following a cardiac arrest. He casually declares her dead, informing the sister. When Mark and Kate discover a faint pulse and start resuscitation, the sister is horrified. Jack covers up, blaming the nurses. Jack and George continue to argue.

An absentee father tries to make friends with his teenage daughter by dancing at a rave club and popping pills. She gives him Ketamine rather than Ecstasy to shock him and make him disapprove. When he collapses and is taken to A&E they both realize that they need to stop acting up to each other and be more honest.

Jack mistakenly tells an elderly lady that her sister is dead — an error which has repercussions for him later on in the series.

Relatives of the woman wrongly declared dead have complained to Elliot. Both Jack and Charlie make statements, but Charlie is puzzled by Jack's version of events.

Guy, a bisexual now living with a girlfriend, is stalked by a male former lover. Guy ends up running over his ex-lover, and has to face up to his sexuality.

A young Asian couple are about to have a baby. The wife wants her mother-in-law to move out of the flat to make a room for the baby. The mother-in-law finds her burning her bedroom curtains; in the ensuing scuffle the wife is badly burned. At A&E, Baz persuades her to try and be reconciled with her mother-in-law.

EPISODE 8
Finders Keepers
by JOE BROUGHTON

Liz and Josh stop at a car accident on their way back from another call. Electing to stay with the three injured people, Liz does what she can while waiting for paramedic Penny to arrive. At Casualty the man cannot be saved, but his girlfriend is encouraged to look after his mentally handicapped brother. She initially rejects this idea, as she always wanted the brother put in a home. Eventually she agrees, but says Liz might as well have left them by the roadside for all the good she did in the end.

EPISODE 9
Whatever It Takes
by TONY LINDSAY

An injured seventeen-year-old girl is brought into A&E by an older woman with a baby. Kate discovers that the baby is the girl's. The other woman and her husband had paid her to have their baby, but she could not give it up.

Kate's anxieties reach a peak when she is discovered shoplifting. Although Charlie begs her to stay, she is determined that the best thing for her to do is to leave Holby.

Kate's shoplifting is reported in the local papers; she goes into work for her last ever shift. In the course of the day she concludes that she has spent her life caring for others and it is time to do something for herself. Horrified by the prospect of losing her, Charlie asks her to come on holiday with him and Baz, but her mind is made up. Elliot fears bad publicity for the hospital but is sympathetic, trying to persuade Kate to have counselling.

EPISODE 10
A Taste of Freedom
by SHELAGH STEPHENSON

A distracted Jack is grateful to Charlie for standing by him in the case of the woman he wrongly certified dead. A woman obsessed with alternative medicine comes in with a cerebral aneurysm; Richard, drawing on his own experience of chronic genetic conditions, persuades her to have an operation.

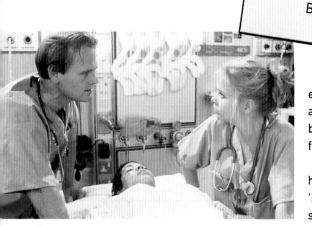

EPISODE 11
Bad Company
by ROBIN MUKHERJEE

SHO George Woodman and Consultant Jack Hathaway bicker about the amount of time Dr McCaig is allowed off work. Although Jack knows about Richard's MS, he keeps George in the dark and she resents having to cover for an absent Richard.

A young woman lives with her boyfriend. She refuses to help her younger brother, who is in care. They all end up arguing in the car, which crashes. The boyfriend dies and the woman's anger intensifies. Jack persuades her that she cannot stop caring for her brother. And he in turn realizes that he must track down his pregnant ex-fiancée, who recently left him, and be with her when their baby is born.

Single mother Christine is injured when she intervenes in a fight between her vicar father and a beggar. Her mother had been passing money to the 'beggar' to give to Christine. Christine's condition suddenly deteriorates, and she dies. The parents are left bereft, reconciled only by their grandson.

It is Liz's last day, which Josh finds hard to accept. It is only when Liz puts her life on the line to save a woman and her son from almost certain death at the hands of a violently possessive husband that Josh realizes he must let go and allow Liz to move on.

Baz and Charlie frantically try to get ready for their holiday, but tensions in the department take their toll and Baz heads off for the airport alone, leaving Charlie at home, bunch of flowers in one hand and ticket in the other.

And a desperately lonely asthmatic sufferer learns from a fellow patient that there is more to life than just having a family around you.

EPISODE 12
Moving On
by JONATHAN RICH

Penny rushes a youth into A&E when he is found unconscious after a training session on a race track. It transpires that he has been injecting himself with insulin in order to improve his performance. His older brother has been pushing him too hard to succeed as an athlete, as he was not good enough himself.

Eve Montgomery arrives on the shift as a temporary replacement for Kate.

A distraught woman rushes into A&E with abdominal cramps, and miscarries on arrival. It is her sixth miscarriage, and Richard helps her explain to her husband that she feels it is so traumatic that she wants to stop trying for a baby altogether.

EPISODE 13
The Power of Persuasion
by TONY LINDSAY

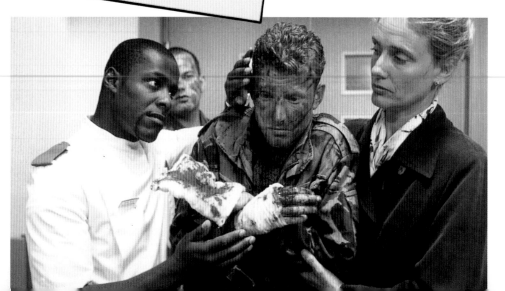

Newcomer Eve is a temporary replacement for Kate. Straight-talking and sometimes brusque, she isn't always easy to work with but the staff at Holby discover that her heart is in the right place.

Mark is rightly concerned that Archie, the locum consultant, is not up to the job. George and Richard wish they were looking after the department themselves.

A bride-to-be argues with her fiancé when he fails to turn up for the vaccinations needed for their Caribbean wedding. He cuts his head, and in Casualty panics when he needs an injection; the bride is relieved that it is the needles he has an aversion to, not her.

A father argues with his son's teacher when the boy is excluded from school. The boy is injured in the fray. In A&E, Mark and Eve have to keep the father and teacher apart. After a few critical moments in resusc., the boy's life is saved, and Mark discovers the warring pair were rivals in the past.

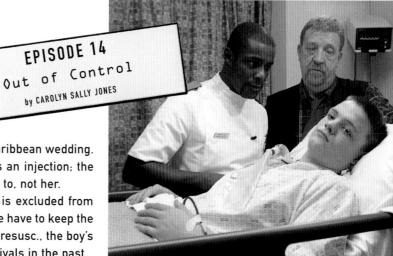

EPISODE 14
Out of Control
by CAROLYN SALLY JONES

Mark sorts out another sticky situation when a row between a teacher and a boy's father results in the boy coming close to death.

EPISODE 15
Love's Labour
by GIL BRAILEY

Baz finds it very hard going back to work after a holiday. She treats a woman prisoner in her thirties, who slashed her arm after her fourteen-year-old lover finished their relationship. Baz discovers that she is heavily pregnant. The young lover turns up at the hospital after all, but the woman's condition worsens and she dies after Baz has performed an emergency caesarean. The terrified new father runs off.

Sam discovers that a patient's broken toe was caused when he kicked a wall in anger, having found out his brother is gay. When the man realizes that Sam too is gay he demands to be treated by another nurse. The two are reconciled when Sam discovers that it is fear of abandonment that drives the man's prejudice.

Josh risks life and limb to rescue a boy called Liam from a fire. Liam's father dies; the man's fiancée thinks Liam started the fire to deliberately scupper the wedding. Josh, only too aware of being left alone as a result of a fire, forms a close bond with Liam and promises to look out for him.

EPISODE 16
Facing Up
by JONATHAN RICH

Charlie, Elliot, personnel officer Zoe and Baz preside over interviews for the G Grade nursing job. They are very impressed with Eve, but Mark misinterprets an innocent question as criticism of his past and breaks down. At the Christmas party it is announced that Eve has got the job. Mark seeks solace in alcohol, and is soon in a passionate embrace with George, watched by a jealous Richard. Charlie's flirtatious friendship with Zoe strains his relationship with Baz more than ever.

Staff go wild at the Christmas party (CENTRE) which leads to some interesting consequences (BOTTOM).

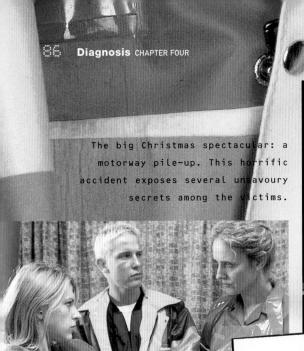

The big Christmas spectacular: a motorway pile-up. This horrific accident exposes several unsavoury secrets among the victims.

When Sam meets the girl his boyfriend is dating, Eve has to pick up the pieces.

EPISODE 17
The Golden Hour
by BARBARA MACHIN

The staff of Holby City A&E are pushed to the limit when a motorway pile-up escalates. A woman on slimming tablets to please her bullying partner has a dizzy spell while driving her car. She skids out of control, and other vehicles crash into her, including a car carrying a quarrelling couple in their thirties who are struggling to maintain their farm; the man is driving a lorry to earn more money when he crashes into the pile-up. The distraught woman wishes she had accepted his proposal of marriage; unfortunately it is too late and he dies due to severe burns.

Mark, George and Sam are with the paramedics attending the injured. Elliot is also along as an observer, and he wants to help. He sees the lorry driver rescue a girl and then fall back into the flames. Elliot and Mark rush through the smoke and succeed in getting him out, but he is severely burned and dies in resusc. When the rescued girl turns out to be seeing Sam's boyfriend, Eve comforts Sam and the animosity previously between them vanishes.

EPISODE 18
An Eye for an Eye
by TONY LINDSAY

After a power failure, the A&E is plunged into semi-darkness. Exasperated with Elliot's lack of leadership, Charlie takes over and does a superb job orchestrating the closure of the department.

George and Mark's relationship is going well until she snaps at him. But she melts when she sees Mark playing with her son Tom.

Baz is absent from the shift because she and Charlie have split up. When Eve realizes this, she suggests that Charlie should draw on the support of his colleagues. He is surprised at her kindness. Sam goes to stay with a reluctant Sunny, as he has to leave the flat he shared with his boyfriend.

A man enters A&E convinced he sustained burns when he made contact with an alien spaceship. Sam and Sunny are happy to dismiss him as a nutter; until, that is, the lights go out and his eyes glow a luminous green.

George can't help but be impressed with Mark's wonderful way with her son Tom.

A mature student is broke and is persuaded to try prostitution. She takes 'speed' to calm her down on her first 'job' and collapses. In Casualty, Baz attempts to make her see sense, but she refuses to listen.

A man is shot in a gang attack; as he is dying he makes Charlie and Baz witnesses to the identity of the man who shot him.

Mark and George are very together and, despite George's misgivings, they reveal their relationship. However, at the end of the shift Mark's ex-girlfriend Laura appears with Jade, a daughter Mark didn't know he had.

Josh wants to help Liam, the young fatherless boy, but Penny is disapproving. Elliot rings Charlie to tell him he is taking emergency leave. And Amy arranges for Tina to go on a blind date with Sunny.

> ### EPISODE 19
> ### Loco Parentis
> *by* ANDREW HOLDEN

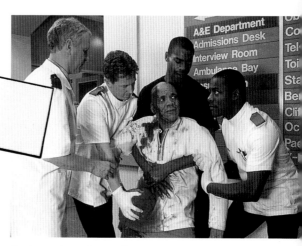

Paul Barber from *The Full Monty* keeps his clothes on for a role as a man shot during gang warfare.

A lthough Baz and Charlie seem temporarily to be reconciled, Charlie is having second thoughts and moves out of their house. Mark is in a state of confusion with the arrival of his ex-girlfriend and daughter and needs time to sort himself out. George is furious with herself for letting him get close. Elliot is suffering post-traumatic stress following the horror of the motorway pile-up.

Tina befriends a man called White, whose wife has been in an accident and will now probably be in a wheelchair for life. She explains what the accident will mean to him. The marriage was an unhappy one anyway, and White becomes unhinged, taking out his frustrations by raping Tina in the hospital.

> ### EPISODE 20
> ### Degrees of Separation
> *by* GIL BRAILEY

As Mark meets the daughter he never knew he had by his ex-girlfriend, George wishes she hadn't let herself become involved with him.

EPISODE 21
Secrets
by JONATHAN RICH

Tina manages to go into work, despite the attack. Sam notices bruising on her wrist and in a panic she says she was mugged. Elliot's tetchy manner continues to rile staff, and no one realizes his state until he breaks down in resusc. Charlie offers to arrange counselling for him.

An increasingly unhappy Liam tries to get Josh's attention with 999 hoax calls. Despite his anger, Josh agrees to arrange a five-a-side football match to raise money for the children's home.

George has an awkward encounter with Laura and Jade, and Richard's attempts to give her some support backfire. Richard is also suffering MS symptoms and goes home early. When George turns up at his house to apologize, he tells her about his MS.

Charlie is miserable at his split with Baz and unexpectedly succumbs to the sexual advances of personnel officer Zoe.

EPISODE 22
Love Me Tender
by TONY LINDSAY

When a mugging victim is brought into Casualty, Tina comes unstuck. Eve asks her to help the woman to the ladies' as her ribs are fractured. Tina is unable to help the woman, and Eve challenges her over her behaviour. Tina breaks down and tells her that she was raped in the ladies' toilets in the hospital. Eve is horrified and takes Tina home. With Tina's blessing Charlie informs the department. Everyone is shell-shocked.

The mugging victim is soon discovered to be Sunny's sister Karen. Sunny confronts her boyfriend who, he is sure, is the one who attacked her. The boyfriend goads him with the fact that Karen will turn against Sunny if he hits him. Sam intervenes and tries to calm Sunny down.

EPISODE 23
Taking Sides
by STEVE CHAMBERS

It is Tina's first day back at work. Eve helps her through it, and persuades her to talk to the police.

Josh's charity football match is a success, but they do not make quite enough money; Josh quietly makes up the difference. Mark discovers that Laura has gone to live with a man who does not want children, leaving Jade in his care. Seeing what Mark is going through, Charlie realizes he cannot bear the thought of life without Baz.

Unlicensed female boxers fight, and one is knocked out. Sam is caught in the middle when they continue fighting at the A&E. The injured one is kicked in the guts and starts to miscarry.

EPISODE 24
We Can Be Heroes
by JONATHAN RICH

Baz is kidnapped at gunpoint by a man obsessed with finding his wife and child. He holds her in a warehouse, while making demands through a police negotiator. The man himself is injured and Baz persuades him to let her call out Charlie with medical equipment. Charlie turns up and Baz treats the man, but he still refuses to let her go. The police arrive, and in the ensuing stake-out Charlie tells Baz that he loves her, and puts his life on the line to save hers.

Back in A&E, Tina has returned from a police identification parade where she identified White as the man who raped her. Liam turns up with an adoption leaflet for Josh. Penny admits to Josh that she understands the need to belong because she herself was brought up in a home; but she tells him he must put things straight with the boy.

Charlie proposes to Baz, and she accepts.

When Baz is taken hostage, Charlie comes to her rescue. As police lead the kidnapper away, Charlie finally tells Baz that he loves her.

EPISODE 25
Everlasting Love (part 1)
by BARBARA MACHIN

Former colleagues Ash, Megan, Mike and Duffy come back to attend Charlie and Baz's wedding. But an emergency at the hospital means everyone has to return to A&E before Charlie and Baz can actually tie the knot.

One case involves an Asian girl, Lamisha, and her non-Asian boyfriend, Damian, who have run away together as her family insist she must have an arranged marriage to an Asian boy. The two have been on the run pursued by Asian gangsters, including Lamisha's brother. Charlie goes to speak to Damian outside the A&E in an attempt to sort out the situation, but sees him being knocked down by a private ambulance driven by Lamisha's brother; he is himself injured by the reversing vehicle. As the ambulance turns for a final run at the wounded Damian, Charlie lies motionless in its path.

Amy looks nervously at her policeman boyfriend, Keith. How will he react to the news of her pregnancy?

Baz, Megan and Eve lovingly tend to heroic Charlie's wounds.

Baz and Charlie, thwarted at the altar. Will Charlie live to tie the knot?

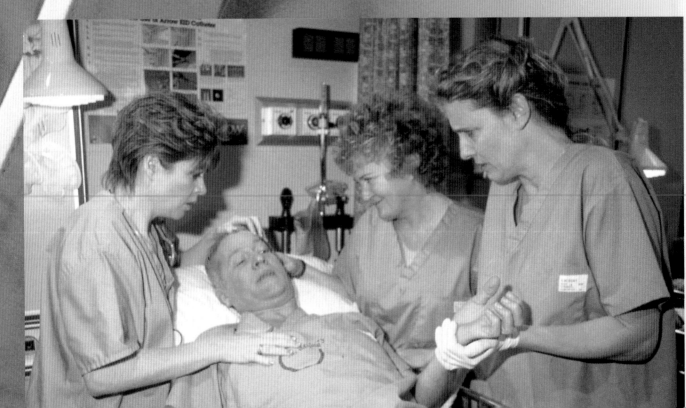

Charlie's life is saved by Josh, who drives straight at the ambulance and diverts it. Charlie and Damian are taken into resusc; their injuries are not serious.

Lamisha explains that her family have put a contract out on Damian. George and Mark urge her to go to the police. But the next time they look in the cubicle the couple have gone. The only way they felt they could survive was on the run.

Finally Baz and Charlie are married on a boat in the Marina, surrounded by all their friends. At the wedding reception Richard decides to leave the department and apply for a research post in Edinburgh; George and Mark get back together; Ash reveals that he and Laura have split up; Amy tells her policeman boyfriend she is pregnant; and Duffy finds a shoulder to cry on in Charlie.

Baz and friends in party mood. Actress Julia Watson chose the wedding outfit herself — the hat from Droopy and Brown, and the tasteful 'not meringuey' suit from Liberty.

Casualty's most volatile couple, the new Mr and Mrs Charlie Fairhead.

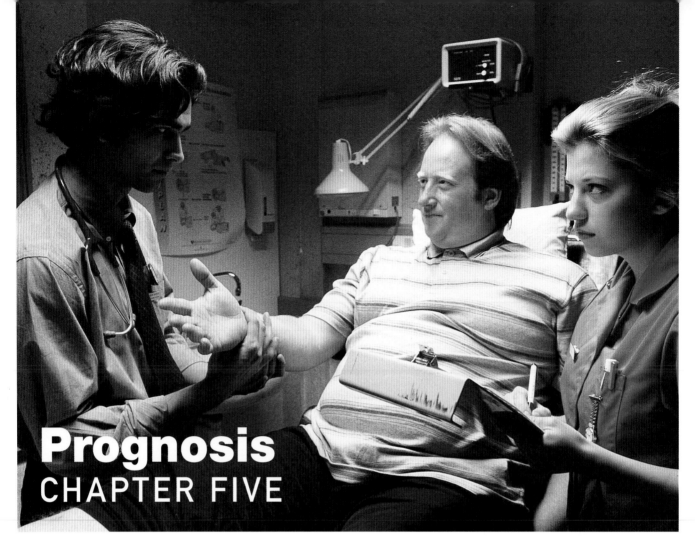

Prognosis
CHAPTER FIVE

Series 13: The Pulse of 1998/99

One of the major issues currently being faced by the Health Service is the amalgamation of the Accident and Emergency departments. On the one hand, consolidation of resources will mean better facilities at each A&E department, but on the other hand it will make them less local. Series producer Johnathan Young and his writers and researchers are now grappling with such issues.

At the same time they have not been neglecting the personal lives of staff at Holby City. This year there will be several new regular characters: the new Consultant Max Gallagher (Robert Gwilym), SHO Sean Maddox (Gerald Kyd), D Grade nurse Chloe Hill (Jan Anderson) and Adam Osman (Pal Aron) who takes up the post of Bed Manager.

Charlie and Baz were married in series 12, but are both secretly relieved when Baz is offered a good position in a Birmingham hospital. This will ease some of their professional complications, and Charlie can commute at weekends.

During rehearsal a *Casualty* camera operator stands in for an 'injured' extra (or supporting artist as they are usually called). Gerald Kyd, who plays new SHO Sean Maddox, and Claire Goose, who returns as nurse Tina Seabrook in series 13, rehearse their medical examination of the patient.

Despite initial reservations, Charlie is beginning to work closely with Max to try and improve the management of A&E and is lobbying hard for its position generally within the hospital trust. As Charlie gradually begins to realize that he is happier and more relaxed at work than he has been for some time, things start to get complicated.

Giving a strong boost to Mark's skill and confidence, Max encourages him to become a Nurse Practitioner. This gives Mark the chance to follow patients right through A&E, and enjoy the special, closer relationship with the patients that develops. This though inevitably gets him into trouble.

Mark and George are still interested in each other, but do not want to commit to anything more permanent for

'Joe', the victim of school bullies, complains he has a stomach ache and begs his dad to excuse him from school. However, later in the episode Joe becomes a school hero after rescuing his classmates from the terrible fire that envelops their school.

the moment. He respects George's wish that they be just friends, but cannot get her out of his system. Just when things seem to be looking up for them, George's ex-boyfriend Martin arrives back on the scene, demanding access to his child and threatening to sue for custody.

Normally philosophical about such matters, Sam is galvanized into action over the overcrowding in A&E following a particularly stressful shift and the brusque manner of Adam, the Bed Manager. But to be fair to Adam,

Lorry driver Gary is rushed by paramedics to resusc. at Holby City A&E after smashing his lorry into a fast-response vehicle when he is distracted by a call on his mobile phone.

his job is one of the toughest in the hospital. There are more patients than beds, and it is the Bed Manager who has to deal with it, putting up with flak from all sides. It is some time before Sam and Adam can become friends.

Tina and newcomer nurse Chloe Hill are colleagues who soon become the best of friends.

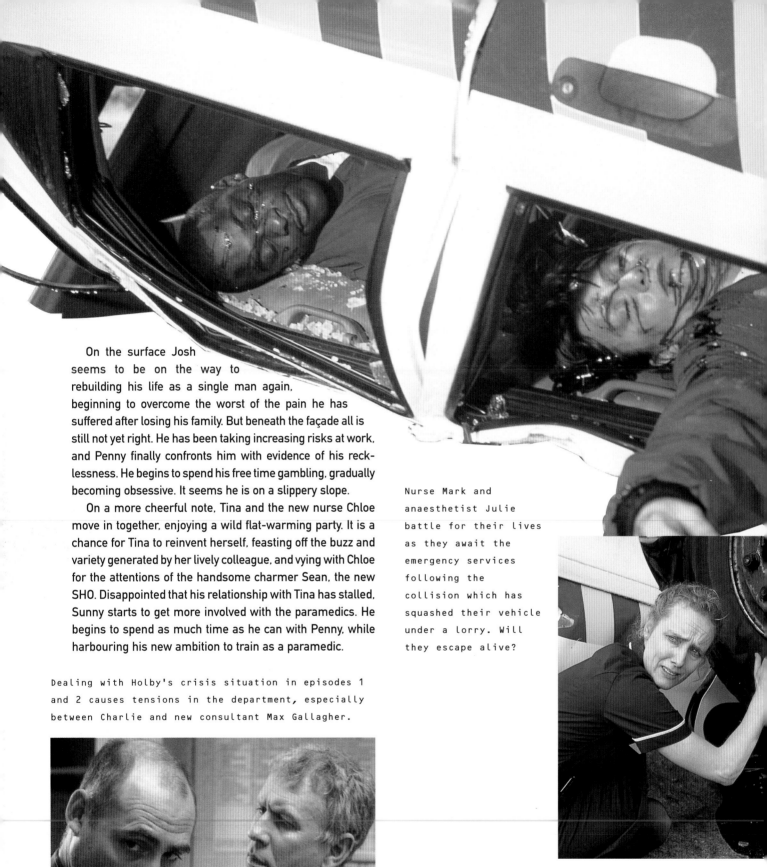

On the surface Josh seems to be on the way to rebuilding his life as a single man again, beginning to overcome the worst of the pain he has suffered after losing his family. But beneath the façade all is still not yet right. He has been taking increasing risks at work, and Penny finally confronts him with evidence of his reck-lessness. He begins to spend his free time gambling, gradually becoming obsessive. It seems he is on a slippery slope.

On a more cheerful note, Tina and the new nurse Chloe move in together, enjoying a wild flat-warming party. It is a chance for Tina to reinvent herself, feasting off the buzz and variety generated by her lively colleague, and vying with Chloe for the attentions of the handsome charmer Sean, the new SHO. Disappointed that his relationship with Tina has stalled, Sunny starts to get more involved with the paramedics. He begins to spend as much time as he can with Penny, while harbouring his new ambition to train as a paramedic.

Nurse Mark and anaesthetist Julie battle for their lives as they await the emergency services following the collision which has squashed their vehicle under a lorry. Will they escape alive?

Dealing with Holby's crisis situation in episodes 1 and 2 causes tensions in the department, especially between Charlie and new consultant Max Gallagher.

Whilst waiting for the fire service to free the trapped staff, Eve keeps talking to Mark, hoping that the sound of a friendly voice will help keep him conscious and alive.

New Bed Manager Adam Osman has a tough time in series 13. Here George and Charlie urgently demand more beds for waiting patients from the already harassed Adam.

Writer Barbara Machin explains her view: 'Every new production team that comes on board *Casualty* challenges the structure. They create new effects, and renew the parameters of the programme.' In her episode there will not be a scene where we do not see Charlie or at least events observed from his point of view. 'It will create a pacy and remorseless portrait of a day in Casualty,' she says. 'The overall hope is that the audience barely notice the new angle; they just see a bloody good episode. We don't want them to get bored, we want them to weep!'

The secrets of another life are revealed when Bonnie, played by Lorraine Chase, is beaten up and arrives for treatment in Casualty. Staff at first suspect that she is a victim of domestic violence, but soon discover that she has been beaten up by a loan shark for not repaying her debts.

Casualty is essentially a patient's eye-view. As an audience we enter the hospital as a patient, and invest emotionally with them. In this new series there will be a chance to observe how the patients look to the doctors and nurses. In one episode we will see an entire day from Charlie's point of view. Material that is not normally dramatic enough to put on to the screen becomes dramatic when you focus on the detail of one character. Johnathan Young describes Charlie as a very potent force in the series: 'It's a bit like mixing black in with colour; you only need a bit of Charlie to absolutely set the agenda within *Casualty*.'

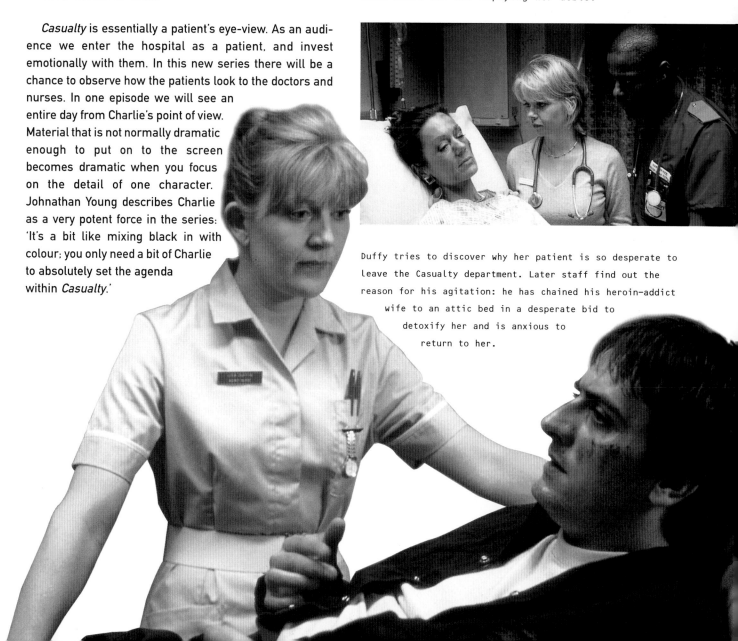

Duffy tries to discover why her patient is so desperate to leave the Casualty department. Later staff find out the reason for his agitation: he has chained his heroin-addict wife to an attic bed in a desperate bid to detoxify her and is anxious to return to her.

Treatment CHAPTER SIX

A great many actors have played their part in making *Casualty* the success it is, becoming firm favourites with viewers in the process. Only Derek Thompson as Charlie has survived through all thirteen series, though Cathy Shipton as Duffy, one of the original characters, makes a welcome return, after a five-year absence, in the new series. Here are some of the familiar characters, along with new ones who'll be making their own mark.

HOLBY HEALTHCARE TRUST

holby
city hospital

Actor: REBECCA LACEY

Character: Dr Georgina Woodman

Doctors

'I love playing George,' enthuses Rebecca Lacey, now in her second year of playing the feisty Senior House Officer. 'She is fiery and competitive and wants to be better than any man. As a former nurse, she sees herself as one of the troops and can't bear anyone from management. It is sheer ambition that has driven her, in her early thirties, to become a doctor and I think she is heading for the top. She sees herself as being very egalitarian and thinks she'd make a wonderful boss!'

The actress feels that George is in control, though she does tend to get into trouble with her sarcastic comments and lack of respect. 'The only reason she doesn't get the sack is because she's such a good doctor.'

As a single parent, bringing up her six-year-old son Tom after his father Martin abandoned her, George is one of life's copers. Her experience, though, does mean that she tends to hold men at arm's length emotionally; only her son can give her unconditional love. Men like

Since her success as the dippy blonde secretary in the long-running BBC comedy *May to December*, Lacey has made sure she has played roles which are as varied as possible. 'I have done some weird, bizarre things, so being cast as George is a relief from some of the mad or emotionally charged women I have played recently.'

HOLBY HEALTHCARE TRUST
holby
city hospital

Actor: JULIA WATSON

Character:
Dr Barbara "Baz" Hayes

Dr Richard McCaig and Staff Nurse Mark Grace find her irresistible, but she has a deep-seated fear of commitment which spills over into her enjoyment of her physical relationship with Mark.

Rebecca Lacey has become fascinated with all the surgical procedures that George must perfect. 'I am very curious, I really need to know what I'm doing with things like chest drains,' she confides with a smile. 'But I do get worried about suturing. The special effects are so good that when I'm supposed to be putting the stitches in I can't see where the make-up ends and the real skin begins. It's just as well I've got a steady hand.'

She doesn't like being recognized too often in the street, and so decided not to wear her off-screen specs for the role, hoping to have something to hide behind. But she has become far too popular for such subterfuge to succeed. 'As it is,' she says, 'I think I may have to have my hair cut really short and dye it red when I finish on *Casualty*!'

Baz Hayes, now Mrs Charlie Fairhead with a two-year-old son, Louis, has been in *Casualty* since it started thirteen years ago. She was then a junior doctor, and was brought back nine years later as a more senior consultant.

'It always amuses me, being cast against type,' laughs actress Julia Watson. 'Baz is a very good and

Strong-willed and ambitious, George can create
conflict between herself and the rest of the staff.

Smiling Baz with baby and father.
How will the family cope in series 13
with spending so much time apart?

competent doctor. When she temporarily becomes head of department she feels very capable of taking control.'

Having spent series 12 coping with the difficulties of juggling a demanding career and family, and also the pressures of working in the same department as her husband, Baz has found a job near her parents in Birmingham to reduce the strain. She believes it will make it easier all round if she and Charlie both have more space at work, and he commutes at weekends.

Watson has endured a similar set-up herself. Her husband, writer David Harsent, and seven-year-old daughter Hannah live in West London, and Watson keeps a flat in Bristol where she stays during the week. If she has to work at the weekend, the family come to stay with her in Bristol.

'If they moved *Casualty* to London it would be perfect: as it is, I know every pothole on the M4. But it's a very good atmosphere on set – we have a great group of regulars and we all get on, which is just as well as we're working together for twelve hours a day.'

The actress appreciates playing a woman who is doing very well in her career and managing a family. 'I get lots of letters from teenagers,' she says. 'Many kids watch, and it is very important to get this positive message across to young women.'

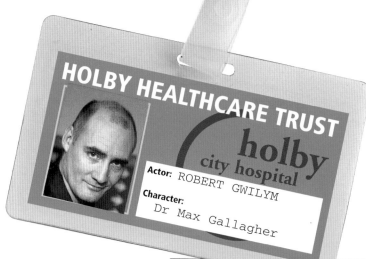

Max Gallagher is the new Consultant and Clinical Director of A&E at Holby City, taking over from Dr Baz Hayes now that she has moved to work near her parents. He is an experienced and dedicated A&E Consultant with huge energy and charisma. In his late forties, he is magnetically attractive, with dark good looks and seductive charm. He's spreading a bit round the middle, but his vague concern about what he puts on the tray in the canteen only adds to his charm.

'You've got to be careful,' laughs actor Robert Gwilym as he pushes away his own lunch plate in the *Casualty* canteen, 'not to put on masses of weight.' Gwilym is originally from South Wales, and now lives in London with his Dutch wife and two children. To research the part of Max, he went to observe the work of medical adviser Phil Coburn in Weston-super-Mare. 'When you actually see people on a hospital trolley the reality of it does does comes home. It was also sobering to see how much damage is self-inflicted: drink, drugs and motorbikes.'

Gwilym sees Max as brimming with confidence at work, but less in control in his personal life. 'He's separated and has a twenty-year-old son who gets into all kinds of trouble. And whereas past consultants have been more public school, Max has a harder edge.'

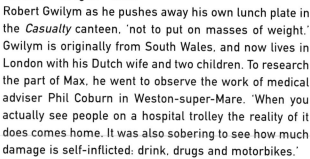

HOLBY HEALTHCARE TRUST

holby city hospital

Actor: GERALD KYD

Character: Dr Sean Maddox

Senior House Officer Sean Maddox is best described as 'a big kid with a life-saving kit'. At twenty-five, he is a beginner at the job, having started work in A&E only a couple of weeks before we meet him. Sean was expelled from practically every school he went to except nursery school and still hasn't learnt his lesson. In his work he always tends to sail pretty close to the wind. It's not that he has a problem with authority – with his over-enthusiasm he simply continuously oversteps the mark. However, he keeps his job with more than youthful charm to recommend him: it's clear that he has the potential to be an extremely good doctor.

```
Flirtatious Dr Sean Maddox tries
out his charm on Chloe.
```

Actor Gerald Kyd was rather nervous when he first took on the part of Dr Sean Maddox; not only did he have to learn all about the medical side of the job, but it was his first television role, having only recently left drama school. In addition to that, Kyd himself is a quiet soul. 'In every scene Sean seems to be chatting up some woman – it doesn't come naturally! Women just like Sean, he doesn't have to try to be liked.'

Sean is no doubt a compulsive flirt, and young nurses like Tina and Chloe love it, enjoying his determination to always have a good time. He is apt to make mistakes, though, and other nursing staff who show him up tend to see him as rather arrogant.

Behind all this there is a sensitive man who, it turns out, knows sign language. His first proper girlfriend was deaf, and he has kept up this knowledge of 'signing' in case she ever has him back.

Nursing Staff

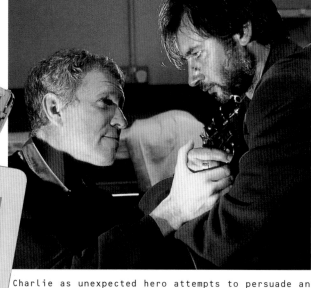

HOLBY HEALTHCARE TRUST

holby
city hospital

Actor: DEREK THOMPSON

Character: Charlie Fairhead

Charlie as unexpected hero attempts to persuade an
armed kidnapper to give up his weapon.

Now that Nurse Manager Charlie Fairhead has married his doctor colleague Baz Hayes, it seems that the tousle-haired unlikely hero has finally come of age. After nearly thirteen years of taking the stress and strain of Holby City firmly on the chin, he apparently has a solid family behind him to relieve some of the pressure.

Alas, it was not to be. Baz has decided that she needs a break from the claustrophobia of working in the same A&E department, and in the new series she has, without consultation, found herself a job as a senior consultant in Birmingham where her mother will be able to help look after their young son Louis. Charlie is to commute at weekends, and the plan is for him to eventually move up there too. Baz thinks this is a great new start for her married life, but Charlie is amazed that Baz should think he could be uprooted so abruptly from Holby. Even fire-bombs and bullets have never prised Charlie from Casualty at Holby City, and now there is just a hint of a suspicion that he is about to enjoy his regained freedom in A&E without Baz.

Although life in A&E can be very stressful, Charlie wouldn't dream of doing any other job.

'All sorts of new pressures impinge on him,' says actor Derek Thompson gleefully. 'But he does have the chance to be a nurse and get the rubber apron on again. I like the gory stuff.' He adds, possibly living up to his reputation as a rather wackier character than the more straitlaced Charlie, 'I enjoyed all the disasters that befell the staff last season – they were like Satan's custard pies.'

In series 13 we will see him predominantly grafting in the department, at work rather than at play. 'The scripts reflect what is really happening. There's quite a high morale in most hospitals, I believe, but the job gets harder all the time.'

Thompson, originally from Belfast, began in show business as part of a song and dance act with his twin sister Elaine and, via stage school in London and a spell in repertory theatre, went on to tackle major roles in TV and film. Memorably he played a vicious bank robber in the film *The Long Good Friday* with Bob Hoskins and Helen Mirren, also appearing in films such as *Yanks* and *Breaking Glass*. For a time he cornered the market in playing young thugs and, with his soft Belfast accent, played many an IRA soldier.

Now in his forties and living in Bristol with actress Dee Sadler, whom he met when she played a pot-holer he hauled out of a horrible cave in an early episode, and their son Charlie, nine, he says he has never for one moment been bored by the long-running character of Charlie, although he would never exchange places with a real nurse.

'Their starting point is on a different planet from mine. Mine is a juvenile desire for story-telling. But people who can deal with the amount of anxiety and disaster you get in an A&E ward for about eighteen hours a day, five shifts a week, I just thank the Almighty for I could no more do what they do than I could levitate.'

HOLBY HEALTHCARE TRUST

holby
city hospital

Actor: BARBARA MARTEN

Character:
Eve Montgomery

Barbara Marten plays starchy Charge Nurse Eve Montgomery, who joined the staff last year as a temporary nurse but, with her striking efficiency and hard graft, was rapidly propelled to a permanent position.

As Marten says, 'Eve is straight as a die, she speaks as she finds and works hard. She does her very best to help. She's a bit brusque but her heart is in the right place.'

However, with her rather brisk manner, reminiscent of a spinster schoolmistress or earnest missionary, she initially found it hard to gain her colleagues' appreciation and trust, though she was undoubtedly respected. It was only when Staff Nurse Sam is abandoned by his sultry American live-in boyfriend for a woman that he finds he can confide in her and find comfort and warmth. Similarly, Eve suddenly becomes a rock of support and sympathy following Tina's rape ordeal which took place actually inside the department. By the end of series 12 the staff are no longer wishing she would go up in flames like the unfulfilled missionary from *The Jewel in the Crown* but have now taken her to their hearts. She even baked a spectacular house-shaped cake for Tina, Sam and Sunny's new flatwarming, and could be seen beaming beneath a new hat at Charlie and Baz's wedding.

Marten herself relishes the growing depth of Eve's character: 'It's great to be able to develop a part, working on something long-term and being a member of a company.'

However, Eve is secretly drawn to religion. The love of her life to date was an Anglican priest she met in India some years back. They grew very serious about each other, but she surprised herself by rejecting him at the point when the relationship was about to turn sexual. This troubled her for a long time, until she realized that it was the religion rather than the man which had drawn her.

Now moonlighting as a voluntary worker at a church-affiliated refuge for the homeless helps to satisfy a basic spiritual need in her. Increasingly drawn to this type of compassionate work, when she goes out to Romania with a Casualty ambulance she is further engaged. By the time she has returned she has decided to train as a lay preacher.

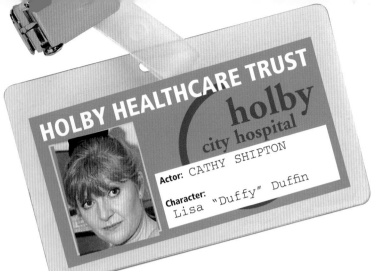

HOLBY HEALTHCARE TRUST

holby
city hospital

Actor: CATHY SHIPTON

Character: Lisa "Duffy" Duffin

In series 13 will nurse Duffy (shown downcast and alone at Baz and Charlie's wedding) be able to keep her marriage alive with husband Dr Andrew Bower?

Staff Nurse Duffy left the department in 1995 when she was pregnant with her second child. Her marriage with the dashing Dr Andrew Bower had been a bit rocky and she felt in need of the time to work on it. Staying home with the kids has been surprisingly tough, and now that her youngest has started school she is more than ready to bounce back. An appearance at Baz and Charlie's wedding left her champing at the bit.

Yo-yo diets, astrological obsessions and all, she leaps back to work, even part-time and as an F Grade nurse when she used to be more senior, with enormous enthusiasm and relief to be back in the swim with her professional colleagues. She's drawn back to A&E because she loved it and because she knows she's good at it. After spending time at home it's great to get back to business.

Having attended the wedding alone at the end of series 12, there is room for concern as to the present state of her marriage, and she has already confided to Charlie that she thinks husband Andrew is bored and cheating on her. Charlie defends him with the plea that husbands can occasionally be fallible – even he fell by the wayside once, a one-night stand with Personnel Manager Zoe.

What is clear is that there is affection between Duffy and Charlie, and perhaps unfinished business.

'It's been strange coming back,' the actress confides. 'Because time has moved on and the gang and the humour have changed. I did feel a bit left out at first but I soon got back into the swing of it.'

Duffy has been doing some agency nursing over the years to keep her up to date, but even so she has to work hard to get back in tune with the others. She also has to deal with the fact that Eve is doing her old job. Eve, however, is not insensitive, and neither of them wants the other staff, particularly Charlie and new consultant Max, to realize that there is anything wrong. But it gradually becomes clear to all that there is a problem.

Cathy Shipton was ready for a change when she left *Casualty* in 1995, after nearly ten years in harness. 'I want to practise my craft out of a blue frock,' she joked at the time. But she was always left scope for return, 'Duffy won't meet a grisly end or anything like that, so she could always come back!'

Shipton lives with actor Christopher Guard, who once played nurse Ken Hodges. She has recently been seen in the Spice Girls movie and on stage with Jenny Eclair in the West End play *Steaming*. Unaccountably, she has also written *The Marathon Book* with athlete Liz McColgan. The ever popular Duffy is back and running.

HOLBY HEALTHCARE TRUST

holby
city hospital

Actor: PATERSON JOSEPH

Character: Mark Grace

Staff Nurse Mark Grace is a man with a mission. He joined the staff in series 12, played by actor Paterson Joseph. 'He is very capable, very positive, and very forth-right,' says the actor. 'He gets involved in the issue of safety for the doctors and nursing staff on Accident and Emergency; violence is a real problem out there. Mark is in the front line when people suddenly lose it, or time-wasters become a nuisance. He steps in and gets physically involved – occasionally when he shouldn't.'

Intelligent and always an academic high-flier, Mark was originally at medical school, getting into the fourth year of his medical degree with flying colours. He formed a special relationship with his senior registrar and was given more and more hands-on surgical opportunities, and encouraged to push himself harder and harder. Doing more and more complex procedural medicine, a mistake was inevitable, and when it came it was disastrous. He started an appendectomy unsupervised and the patient died. The registrar offered to take the rap, but Mark was devastated and left medical school.

In an attempt to teach himself humility, and because he refused to fail at the same thing twice, he decided to leave his past completely behind him and train as a nurse. Although leaving his family was a wrench, blotting out his medical studies was easy, and his past is a mystery to everyone at Holby except Charlie and George.

Mark has a strong sense of fair play and is always one to stand up and be counted at work. Despite being a smoker he is very fit and amazes others by his stamina, after a hard day's nursing and negotiating. Mark is not the type to go home and put his feet up. He loves to go out partying and clubbing.

'He is very involved with the younger members of staff like Sam and Tina,' explains Joseph. 'After the heaviness of his work, he likes to expend himself on the dance floor. Part of him likes to just let loose.'

Of course his life has been complicated, not only by his on-again off-again romance with George (who also had other suitors such as Dr Richard McCaig), but by the reappearance of an old girlfriend, Laura, who turns up with a six-year-old daughter, Jade, Mark never knew he had. Laura wants to go off with a man who does not want children, and so abandons Jade to be cared for by her father. Confused and astounded, Mark is forced into domesticity.

Playing Mark is not Paterson Joseph's first taste of joining a long-running hit series. He spent a blistering hot few months filming a series of *Soldier Soldier* in Cyprus. 'It involved lots of water stunts – and I can't swim,' he grimaces. 'It taught me how to trust inflatables and stunt men.'

Mark and Sam out of uniform at Baz and Charlie's wedding: both these nurses are partial to a good night out on the town.

HOLBY HEALTHCARE TRUST

holby city hospital

Actor: CLAIRE GOOSE

Character: Tina Seabrook

One of his better acting experiences was taking a production of *Hamlet* to New York. 'I played Horatio and it was a very simple, very powerful production. Some incredible names came to see us, and my wife Emmanuelle was out there with me too. It was a golden time, like a second honeymoon.'

Perhaps because of a stint in his student days as a hospital chef, Paterson insists he is not fazed by the acclaimed special effects on *Casualty*. 'I love the blood and guts,' he says with relish. He adored the opening episode of series 12 when he joined the team: 'It involved an explosion in a shopping arcade, especially gory injuries – lots of people with bits of glass sticking out of them.'

Now Nurse Mark Grace is set to progress through the system. He joins the Nurse Practitioner scheme, which gives him more power, allowing him to follow patients right through A&E. Both his skill and enjoyment of the job increase as he is able to develop a special, closer relationship with the patients. New consultant Max is keen for his staff to work to their full potential – though Mark inevitably gets himself into trouble when he gets too close to a female patient. Through all this Mark and George remain emotionally very bound up. George prefers them to remain just friends for a time, but he can never get her out of his system.

Norfolk-born Claire Goose is a doctor's daughter, but she never wanted a career in medicine. 'My dad has been a big help since I got this part, though,' she grins. 'He spent a lot of time on A&E and arranged for me to do some research at the Casualty department in King's Lynn. I felt a fraud walking round in a white coat – people even came up to ask things thinking I was a real doctor. But it was a good experience and helped me with how to play Tina.

'Tina is a real go-getter, a real determined and head-strong girl who can sometimes be a bit like a bull in a china shop. She can get things wrong, but never too drastically. She doesn't kill anyone.'

Tina's parents wanted her to marry young and join the family business, but she had set her sights firmly on nursing and refused to go along with their aspirations. She always did well at school, but never felt driven academically, preferring to get her hands dirty through day-to-day involvement with people. Her parents feel let down by her choice of career. The continuing pressure from her family makes Tina if anything even more determined to succeed.

She is fiercely ambitious, and often forgets quite how much she has to learn, though Charlie keeps an eye on her, realizing that she has the makings of a good nurse. There's nothing Tina likes more than a quick fag and a good laugh. Sam and Tina become friendly, to the extent that her colleagues suspect her of leading him astray.

In series 13 she shares a flat with Sam and Sunny, but though they are all friendly, it gets too complicated, and when a new young nurse, Chloe, joins the A&E, Tina happily moves in with her. It is a chance for Tina to reinvent herself after the trauma of her rape ordeal: she is one of the girls again, gossiping, giggling and partying, nothing is sacred!

Tina enjoys spending time with her new flatmate but is also looking for love and commitment in a relationship with a man. She develops a crush on new Senior House Officer Sean, and though he seems to have an easier rapport with happy-go-lucky Chloe she still is getting some response.

Claire Goose wanted to be an actress from an early age. She joined the Italia Conti stage school at sixteen, desperate to learn as much as she could about acting – though she also had to do three dance classes a day. 'I enjoyed them but I always knew I wanted to do serious acting rather than musical theatre. Since I left, the longest I have been out of work has been six months, but I have never signed on the dole – that's lethal. That's how you end up being really depressed about the whole thing. I made sure I had a life outside acting. Working in a café between jobs kept me sane and stopped me waiting by the phone all day.'

As two of the younger members of staff, Tina and Sam become firm friends at Holby City.

Now in her early twenties, Claire has had parts in *The Bill* and in the BBC Screen 2 film *Loved Up*. Notoriously in *EastEnders* she played the part of the trainee hairdresser responsible for Robbie's hideous highlights. She is also remembered as the back-packing girl who washes her hair in a fountain in a shampoo commercial. When she took part in a *Crimewatch* reconstruction the BBC switchboards were jammed by viewers saying – 'You want the girl from the Wash and Go ad!'.

HOLBY HEALTHCARE TRUST

holby
city hospital

Actor: JONATHAN KERRIGAN

Character: Sam Colloby

Sam grew up in the lively atmosphere of his parents' pub which the family lived above. His father left them when he was only eleven and he grew up quickly, helping his mum at the bar, and generally radiating a hospitable charm. This charm led to some early sexual encounters with men, and he came out as gay when he was only sixteen. Although he was extremely bright, Sam left school early with only a handful of GCSEs, planning to become a famous DJ, having already achieved some notoriety on the club circuit as the 'Sonic Sound Sensation'.

Encouraged by his aunt, Sam volunteered his services as a hospital DJ, and was soon well known in his twice-weekly slot, 'Colloby's Holloby'. Exposure to the traumas of hospital life made a deep impression on him and he was encouraged by the nursing staff to train as a nurse. Sam trained for three years on the nursing 2000 scheme, and his decision to specialize in A&E was governed by his genuine interest in people and his ability to communicate across the generations.

Jonathan Kerrigan who plays Sam also likes music and clubbing. In one episode which had Sam and Mark rolling in from a club at dawn, he hardly had to act, as he had in fact been up until 4 a.m. at a party to judge the Mr Gay UK contest in Birmingham.

Sam's flat is untidy and littered with empty beer cans, particularly when he still lived with his idle American boyfriend in series 12, but in reality Jonathan shares an

Staff Nurse Sam Colloby, 22, is charming, witty and lively. He is relaxed and comfortable about being gay, although his Aunt Eileen remains the only person in his family who is ignorant of his sexuality and thinks he'll make some lucky woman a lovely husband. Physically he is attractive and athletic. While he is no fashion victim, he has his own distinctive style.

Sam helps out in series 13 as new SHO Sean examines a patient who has been rushed in unconscious due to smoke inhalation in a major fire.

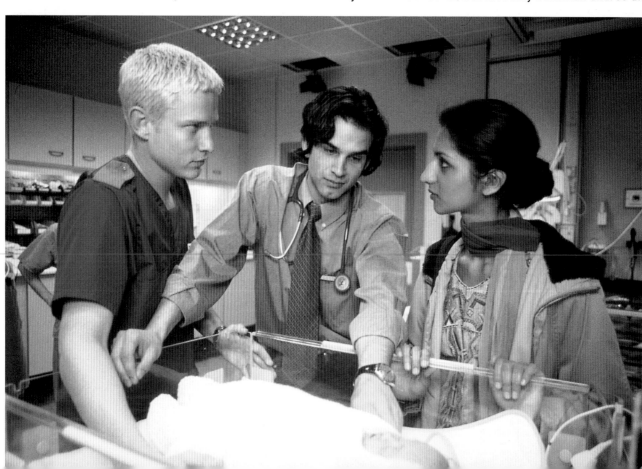

immaculately tidy pad with fellow *Casualty* actor Vincenzo Pellegrino who plays porter Sunny. 'Being of Italian descent, Vince is a great cook, so the kitchen's his department. It's all very civilized. The other night we were sitting with the candles lit and I was composing music and Vince was writing poetry; not *Men Behaving Badly* at all.'

As a 'straight' person, Jonathan is delighted that Sam is believable, 'I know that there have been gay characters on television before, but with Sam there is no shock, no trauma, he's just out having a laugh.'

Having landed the part in *Casualty* straight from Leeds University, Jonathan is feeling confident; he even finds himself being considered for film roles.
Both Sam and Jonathan seem to
have landed on their feet.

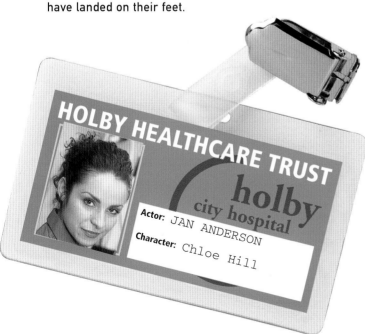

HOLBY HEALTHCARE TRUST

holby
city hospital

Actor: JAN ANDERSON
Character: Chloe Hill

Chloe Hill is the newest nurse on A&E. Young and friendly, energetic and optimistic, she loves to have a good time. Just the tonic that Tina needs, the two girls become firm friends.

She grew up in the inner city, with parents who were also foster parents to any number of children at a time. As a consequence although Chloe likes people, and is used to mixing with people from all walks of life, she can err towards the self-centred, having had to battle for every bit of attention she could get at home.

An extrovert herself, the bubbly actress Jan Anderson has been an actress and dancer since she left school at fifteen to tour with the Welsh National Opera. She moved to London a year later, and has been working consistently on stage and television ever since, recently appearing in the feature film *Human Traffic* which previewed at Cannes. Anderson loves a lively night life, finding Bristol a bit quiet after her flat in 'wicked' Notting Hill Gate.

In the latest series, Chloe's cheeky personality livens things up at Holby.

Similarly Chloe is a hedonist, but doesn't know when to stop or say no. Partying all night when she is not actually on shift, she loves drinking and boy bands. The boys see her as the original babe. Despite all this, she has chosen to be in a profession where she is dedicated to helping people. She is perfectly aware of this contradiction but has decided not to even try and rationalize it; she simply brushes aside any thought that there could be a problem. The older nurses wisely put it down to her extreme youth.

'You only live once,' is the maxim Chloe lives by and from her entry into A&E, where she adores the buzz and variety, at the beginning of series 13 she gets down to the crucial business of dating policeman Pat, and flirting with the attractive new Senior House Officer, Sean.

The Paramedics

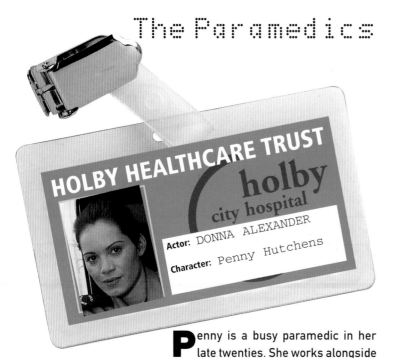

Penny is a busy paramedic in her late twenties. She works alongside Josh, and respects his professional skills, but is not sure she likes him. Penny has a passion for boyish concerns, such as football and motorbikes. She met most of her friends through football, and they meet up in her local pub to discuss tactics and promotions for their beloved team. When Josh gets a team together to play a charity match in aid of the local children's home, she pushes herself forward as the only female player. Meanwhile in the pub she can down pints with the best of them.

Having grown up in a children's home in Oldham, Penny finds it quite disturbing when Josh takes an interest in a boy, Liam, who has been orphaned in an accident and is now living in a local children's home. She finds herself forced to relive unpleasant, lonely memories.

On the brighter side, when she left the home at sixteen she was welcomed into the bosom of a surrogate family. She still lives with 'Mo', Maureen, the mother of the family, now that Maureen is on her own. Mo cooks for her every night as if she were feeding a large family and it is only Penny's high metabolism and active job that enable her to cope with the consistent supply of hearty meals.

Josh and Penny start to get competitive at work, which can be a strain, mitigated only by the unexpected attentions of Sunny, a much less complex character. She feels flattered by Sunny's devotion, and begins to relax and enjoy it.

Now in his mid forties, Ian Bleasdale has been playing Josh the paramedic at Holby City since 1989, and is so convincing that it is widely held that he thinks he really is a paramedic! However, the Lancashire-born former teacher found the realities he saw while researching a paramedic's job hard to swallow. 'I certainly couldn't do it for real,' he said at the time. 'Playing Josh has given me confidence that I could cope with the first aid, the "there, theres", even the overdoses, strokes and falls. But dealing with the relatives is just too tough.' None the less, he talks of 'we' paramedics as though born to the job.

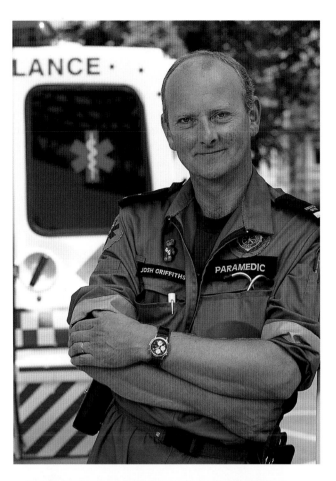

Josh is funny, good-humoured and sensitive and although he doesn't often show it, he feels things deeply. He is highly trained and intelligent, and his quick thinking has helped save countless lives over the years, and his patience and dedication have also helped previous partners, like Liz Harker, to become first-class paramedics.

He was devoted to his wife and two daughters, one of whom was wheelchair-bound as she had cystic fibrosis. When they were killed in a house fire he was devastated, but to some extent buried his grief. It was only through the persistence of his former ambulance partner Liz that he was able to let out some of the pain.

Josh still misses his family terribly, and although on the surface he seems to be rebuilding his life, the emotion begins to seep out in other guises. Josh has been taking increasing risks in his job, and it is only when Penny eventually confronts him that he realizes how reckless he has become. When he stops taking the risks at work, however, he finds an outlet in gambling, soon acquiring an obsessive streak. It is only when he has lost nearly everything that he can see what he is doing, and begin to put his life back on track.

Josh still saving lives after the shockingly tragic deaths of his wife and two children in series 11. Here he attends to the injured after a school goes up in flames.

Other Principals

HOLBY HEALTHCARE TRUST
holby city hospital
Actor: REBECCA WHEATLEY
Character: Amy Howard

Actress Rebecca Wheatley, who plays A&E receptionist Amy, is best known for her singing when away from the *Casualty* set in Bristol. She has spent much of her career on London's club scene as well as touring with shows such as *Godspell* and *Cabaret*.

Recently she took over the lead in the cabaret *All Aboard* at Madame JoJo's, Soho's celebrated nightspot, where all the glamorous 'hostesses' are in drag. 'It was great fun and the costumes were amazing, but it meant being squashed into a tiny dressing room worrying about the size of my eyelashes and finishing work at four in the morning. Playing Amy is a bit of a change.'

However, Amy does have a real zest for life, and a large group of friends who love nothing better than a wild day out at Alton Towers screaming on all the roller coasters, or piling down to the beach for a picnic. 'She is lots of fun. She's vivacious and larger than life and can be quite flirtatious – I think she goes out and about with musicians. She is certainly no wallflower and sometimes favours a rather nice lime green skirt. But she doesn't quite live up to my off-screen outfits.'

The busy reception desk at A&E is a haven for youngsters under Amy's ministrations; she keeps a large jar of sweets on the counter. This means that

Rebecca has had to do that dreaded thing: work with children. 'Amy has a bit of a fixation with children. She always gravitates towards them if there are any in the waiting area and gets on with them very well. I like kids too and one scene with a clown was great to do. There were about fifteen children and they all had a lovely time. But another scene was a bit of a disaster. I had rehearsed over and over with this little boy, he was only about two and a half, and everything had gone fine. But when it came to do it for real he went and hid under the table – and nothing would bring him out. I tried everything, bribing him with sweets and lollipops, but he wasn't having it.'

It is perhaps fortunate for Wheatley that she has gained all this experience with children, now that Amy has announced that she is pregnant by her boyfriend, policeman Keith. She is keeping the baby even though she is not sure whether the father will stick around. Due in January, there is much excitement at the thought of another *Casualty* birth.

HOLBY HEALTHCARE TRUST

holby
city hospital

Actor: VINCENZO PELLEGRINO

Character: Derek "Sunny" Sunderland

A&E porter Sunny, twenty-six, can be a real distraction in the department, and is often so entertaining that he stops staff from getting on with their jobs. But he is certainly a ray of sunshine, with his ready smile and cheery quips.

'He is pretty bright in his own way,' says Pellegrino. 'In fact I see him as a kind of Cassandra figure. He sees everything that is going on and warns everyone about what is going to happen, but no one believes him.'

To prepare for his role, Vincenzo spent time with the real thing. 'A lot of the young porters I spoke to certainly don't want to be doing it for the rest of their lives. They have a sense of lack of achievement because the hospital hierarchy is extremely apparent – and porters are seen as the bottom of the heap.'

In fact, now that Tina has made it clear she is not interested in him, Sunny has begun to get involved with the paramedics. He spends as much time as he can with Penny – partly an interest in her and partly a genuine desire to become a paramedic.

After training at Manchester School of Theatre, Pellegrino got a part in the Jimmy Nail series *Crocodile Shoes*. In Manchester he also shone at music, and was voted best bongo player in the city's Battle of the Bands. Now he shares a flat in Bristol with Jonathan Kerrigan who plays Sam. 'We have a good time. I may even splash out on a new set of drums – that should please the neighbours!'

Cheeky 'Sunny' puts 'missing' posters of Eliott up in the department for a joke after Eliott goes AWOL due to post traumatic shock syndrome. Charlie is not amused.

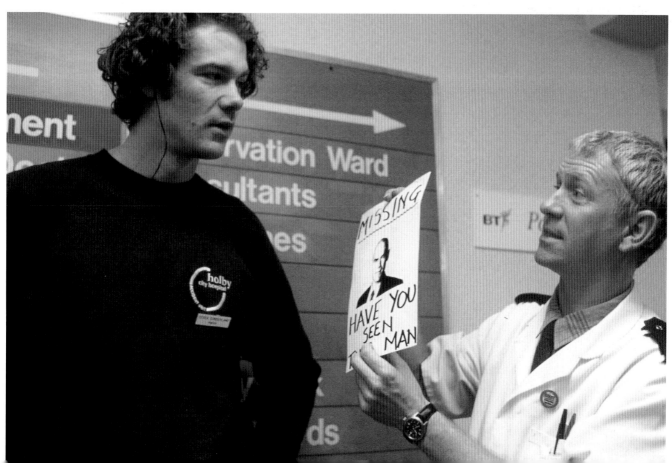

The Clinical Team 1995–1999

PAL ARON
(Adam Osman)

PETER BIRCH
(Jack Hathaway)

LISA COLEMA
(Jude Kocarn

DONNA ALEXANDER
(Penny Hutchens)

JAN ANDERSON
(Chloe Hill)

IAN BLEASDALE
(Josh Griffiths)

ROBERT GWILYM
(Max Gallagher)

PATERSON JOSEPH
(Mark Grace)

JONATHAN KERRIGAN
(Sam Colloby)

MICHAEL N. HARBOUR
(Trevor Wilson)

CRAIG KELLY
(Dr Daniel Perryman)

PATRICK ROBINSON
(Martin `Ash` Ashford)

CATHERINE SHIPTON
(Lisa `Duffy` Duffin)

DEREK THOMPSON
(Charlie Fairhead)

SUE DEVANEY
(Liz Harker)

GANIAT KASUMO
(Gloria Hammond)

JANE GURNETT
(Rachel Longworth)

SORCHA CUSACK
(Kate Wilson)

ROBERT DUNCAN
(Peter Hayes)

PETER GUINNESS
(Elliot Matthews)

CLAIRE GOOSE
(Tina Seabrook)

REBECCA LACEY
(Dr Georgina Woodman)

BARBARA MARTEN
(Eve Montgomery)

VINCENZO PELLEGRINO
(Derek 'Sunny'
Sunderland)

JASON MERRELLS
(Matt Hawley)

KYD
n Maddox)

CLIVE MANTLE
(Mike Barratt)

GRAY O'BRIEN
(Dr Richard McCaig)

LIZZIE McINNERNY
(Laura Milburn)

JULIA WATSON
(Barbara 'Baz' Hayes)

REBECCA WHEATLEY
(Amy Howard)

Who Loves Who in Casualty?

Romance is one of the powerful themes that attracts millions of viewers to *Casualty* every Saturday night. Relationships abound – some affairs merely flirtations, others leading to marriage. One or two couples even eloped.

LEFT Peter Hayes, Baz Hayes and Charlie Fairhead, the series 10 love triangle. Baz and Charlie were lovers when they worked together in series 9 and the spark is rekindled when Baz returns to Holby following her marriage to Peter. After long and fraught deliberations, Baz puts Charlie out of his misery and leaves her husband for him.

RIGHT Charlie and nurse Lisa 'Duffy' Duffin, who makes a return to *Casualty* in series 13, have been close friends in the past. Now that Baz is working in Birmingham, will they use this opportunity to develop a dangerously close relationship?

RIGHT Charlie's flirtatious relationship with Zoe, the hospital Personnel Officer, strains his relationship with Baz more than ever. Still in love with Baz, he regrets allowing himself to be seduced over cocktails and the one-night stand is not repeated.

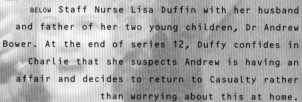

BELOW Staff Nurse Lisa Duffin with her husband and father of her two young children, Dr Andrew Bower. At the end of series 12, Duffy confides in Charlie that she suspects Andrew is having an affair and decides to return to Casualty rather than worrying about this at home.

ABOVE Receptionist Matt Hawley with nurse Jude Kocarnick. Following Jude's recovery from her stabbing at the end of series 11 and the realization that they are both in love with each other, the couple get married in Crete.

SHO Dr Richard McCaig has a flirtation with nurse Gloria Hammond in series 11 which unfortunately comes to nothing — they part before the series ends.

Former Consultant Mike Barratt and nurse Rachel Longworth leave the hospital quietly together towards the end of series 10 to do relief work in Somalia.

A really happy couple. Actors Lizzie McInnerny and Patrick Robinson play the parts of Public Relations Officer Laura Milburn and Martin 'Ash' Ashford.

The famous series 12 love triangle: nurse Mark Grace, SHO 'George' Woodman and SHO Richard McCaig. At the end of series 12, Richard reveals that he is to start working in Edinburgh and steps out of the 'contest'. Shortly after, Mark and George are seen leaving together after Baz and Charlie's reception.

'Best of' Series Endings

Series 8 'Cascade'

BY GINNIE HALE

An horrific plane crash at Holby airport. A plane full of returning holiday-makers crashes into an embankment. Holby hospital staff are pushed to their limits trying to tend to the many victims.

Series 1 'Closure'

BY JEREMY BROCK

In the final episode of the very first *Casualty* series, Holby City is threatened with closure. Nurses Duffy and Susie demonstrate outside the department but cannot prevent Holby losing its night shift and opening only to minor injuries in the day. All is not lost though, as in series 2 Charlie manages to secure full status for Holby.

Series 11 'Perfect Blue'

BY BARBARA MACHIN

Nurse Jude is found in a hospital corridor covered in blood, victim of a vicious stabbing. Boyfriend, ex-receptionist Matt, rushes back from Crete to be by her side while the other staff wait anxiously in intensive care for a sign that she'll pull through. Luckily, in the next series, Jude makes a full recovery and flies to Crete for her marriage to Matt.

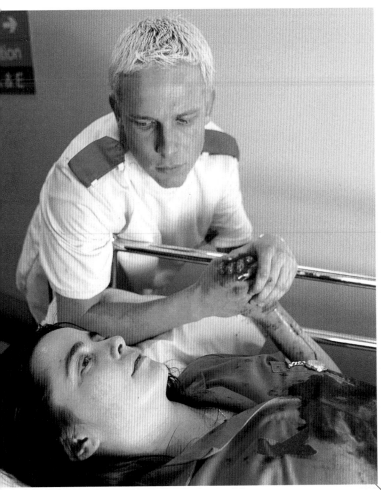

Series 7 'Boiling Point' BY PETER BOWKER

A gang of rioting youths burn down the hospital in this controversial episode and we are left with the cliffhanger 'Will Holby City survive?'

Series 12 'Everlasting Love'

BY BARBARA MACHIN

The 'Wedding of the Year' — Baz and Charlie are married in style on board ship. Even then, we are kept waiting for them to tie the knot: the ceremony is inter-rupted mid-way by a class one Holby emergency. For once out of uniform and dressed to kill, the staff of Holby City A&E break into a spontaneous rendition of 'Everlasting Love' at the reception.

Medical Terms and Jargon

Any aficionado of *Casualty* ought to be up to date with all the medical terms. Authenticity in this department is essential. New script writers are issued with a confidential information pack known as 'The Bible'. Included in this is the following vital glossary which keeps them abreast of the latest medical and slang terminologies.

BID	Brought in Dead; dead for some time before picked up by the ambulance.
Bleeps	Never called 'bleepers'. You dial the bleep number and then the extension you are calling from.
Blood	'Crossmatched' to the patient if time allows. If there is no time to make a match, the patient is given the universal donor, 'O negative'.
Bradycardia	Slow pulse.
Canula	Plastic tube inserted into a vein via a needle to administer intravenous (IV) fluids, drugs or blood. There are various sizes.
Cardiac arrest	The heart stops and needs resuscitation. Not the same as a heart attack. Cardiac arrest rhythms are 'ventricular fibrillation' (VF), a quivering of the heart but no beat, which needs to be treated by a defibrillator, and 'asystole', where the heart is at a standstill. Both show a flat line on a monitor.
Cas officer	Casualty officer – an A&E Doctor/Senior House Officer (SHO).
Crash call	An emergency call to staff to assist with a cardiac arrest.
Coronary or MI	A heart attack, technically known as Myocardial Infarction. There is damage to heart tissue; sections of the heart die off.
C2h or ETOh	Abbreviated chemical terms for alcohol; applied to drunks.
DIC	Died in Casualty.
DKA	Diabetic Keto Acidosis; very high blood sugar.
DOA	Dead on Arrival.
Fluids	Intravenous (IV) fluids; usually 'saline' in the hospital or 'Hartman's' in the ambulance.
Fracture	A broken bone.
GCS	Glasgow Coma Scale: a specific assessment of consciousness as a numerical score: 3 is the lowest – in a coma (or dead drunk); 15 is fully alert.

General, GA	General anaesthetic.
Giving set or lines	Plastic tubes connecting bags of fluid/blood, etc. to the canula.
Going off	Deteriorating.
Hopper	An abuser of the hospital system; someone with Munchausen Syndrome.
Hyper pyrexia	Very high temperature.
Hypo	Hypoglycaemic – having low blood sugar (as in diabetes).
Injections	Can be given three ways: IV (intravenous), IM (intramuscular, arm or leg), SC (subcutaneous, upper arm, leg or abdomen, e.g. for insulin). Nurses can use all sites. Doctors very rarely do IM or SC injections.
Intubation	Insertion of a plastic tube into the trachea to maintain breathing artificially.
Local, LA	Local anaesthetic.
MSU	Mid Stream Urine: routine urine test, carried out after any abdominal pain, when a urinary tract infection is suspected, or with a high temperature.
Neuro obs	Neurological observations: specific set of vital signs for head injuries or unconscious patients.
NOF	Neck of Femur fracture, commonly known as a fractured hip.
Obs	Observations: vital signs, comprising blood pressure (BP), temperature (temp), respiratory rate (resps) and pulse.
Per	A Latin word meaning 'by': p.o. (by mouth), p.v. (by vagina), p.r. (by rectum).
PUO	Pyrexia of Unknown Origin.
Pyrexia	Raised temperature.
Query	Prefix for undiagnosed conditions, e.g. 'query NOF', written as '? NOF'.
Receiver	Kidney dish (not metal these days).
RTA	Road Traffic Accident.
Sphyg	Sphygmomanometer: a manual blood pressure machine (the electronic ones are usually known by their trade names).
Sutures	Stitches, of various types and sizes for wounds.
Tachycardia	Rapid pulse.
Tourniquet	Used to raise veins for a canula, etc. (<u>not</u> to stop bleeding).
UTI	The Ambulance Service use this abbreviation for Under the Influence; drunk. In a hospital these letters mean Urinary Tract Infection.